SPIRIT OF THE
OCEAN

SPIRIT OF THE

OCEAN

Discover the beauty of our underwater world

Daniel Gilpin

PaRragon

Bath New York Singapore Hong Kong Cologne Delhi Melbourne

First published by Parragon in 2007

Parragon
Queen Street House
4 Queen Street
Bath BA1 1HE, UK

ISBN 978-1-4054-9849-4

Printed in China

Designed, produced and packaged by Stonecastle Graphics Limited

Text by Daniel Gilpin
Designed by Paul Turner and Sue Pressley
Edited by Anthony John

Contents

Chapter 1
Where Land Meets Sea

Life on the Edge

The shoreline is a tough place to live. To survive here, animals have to be able to cope with crashing waves, immersion in sea water and exposure to air. As the tides cover and expose them, they experience sudden changes in temperature. What is more, many have two sets of predators to avoid – those that live in the water and those that fly or live on land and breathe air.

The majority of shore creatures are ocean dwellers that have adapted to life in the surf. These animals get their oxygen from water and so potentially face great danger whenever the tide goes out. Some, such as prawns and fish, avoid the problem by retreating with the falling water. A few may find themselves temporarily trapped in rock pools, but as long as they remain surrounded by water they can still breathe until released again by the returning tide.

Other animals have evolved methods to enable them to survive both in and out of the sea. Mudskippers, for example, which live along many shores in the tropics, have gills like other fish but can also absorb oxygen through their skin from the air. This rare ability enables them to venture out on to the land, held upright by their strong pectoral fins, and exploit food resources that are out of reach of other fish.

Most shoreline animals, however, are dependent on water to breathe. The majority of crabs, although perfectly able to move about on land, have to regularly return to the water to top up their oxygen levels. They carry water about with them when on land, held inside their carapaces, but this has to be flushed out and replaced whenever the oxygen in it becomes used up. The idea is much the same as that employed by human SCUBA divers, but in reverse.

Crabs are highly mobile creatures but not all shoreline animals are able to nip in and out of the water when they please. Many are too slow moving or spend their lives attached to one spot. For these creatures, life depends on being able to survive on a little oxygen and conserving the water that contains it until the tide returns.

Right: *The seashore is a dynamic and challenging habitat for living creatures.*

Mussels, for instance, clamp their shells shut just before the falling tide exposes them to the air. By doing this they trap a reservoir of water against their flesh which supplies them with the little oxygen they need until the waves return and they are able to open their shells again. Other shellfish, such as limpets and winkles, pull themselves tight against the rocks for exactly the same reason. As well as keeping them from suffocating, the water also prevents these molluscs from drying out.

Of course, not all shoreline creatures need water to breathe – in fact, for some it is quite the opposite. The many shore birds, which, to our eyes at least, are the most obvious denizens of these habitats, seem to spend a large part of their lives at the water's edge, but avoiding the water itself. The reason for this is not that they are afraid of the water – in fact, with their long legs, most wading birds are perfectly capable of walking through it without getting their feathers wet – but has to do with their food. As the tide recedes, tiny animals are briefly exposed before they burrow into the mud or sand. The few moments when they are still visible are the ones when they are most easy to catch. By following the edge of the water down the shore, the birds are simply concentrating their numbers where they can find the most food.

Below: *Horseshoe crabs leave the sea to lay their eggs on beaches. These primitive creatures are not true crabs at all but are more closely related to spiders.*

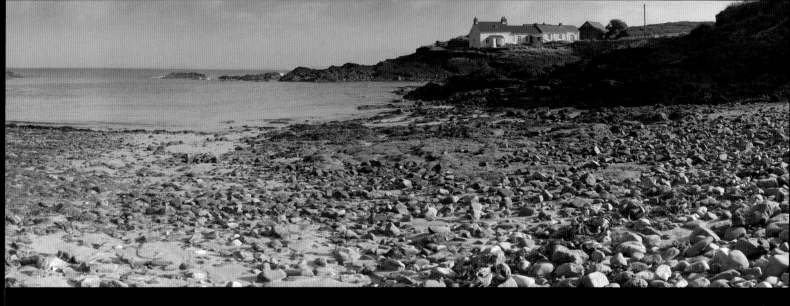

Wading birds, such as godwits, oystercatchers, curlews and turnstones, rely on shoreline habitats to provide them with food. Many other birds find their food at sea but are drawn to the world's coastal habitats in order to nest. Some, such as terns, nest above the high tide line on shingle or sandy beaches but most prefer the predatorproof safety of cliffs. Cliffs have the added advantage of being easy places from which to take off – an important consideration for many diving birds, such as guillemots, which have difficulty getting airborne from the ground.

In spring and summer, sea cliffs around the world become hives of activity, full of noisy nesting colonies of birds. Horizontal space is usually at a premium and even the tiniest ledges are often packed with nests and incubating parents.

On some coasts, the beaches below draw their own seasonal visitors from the sea. Many seals and sea lions gather in such places to have their pups, protected by the cliffs from land predators which might otherwise attack them. Sand banks and island shores are also favoured by these marine mammals for the same reason.

Turtles are also drawn to beaches at certain times of the year. Although they spend their lives at sea, they lay eggs which cannot survive in water, a relic of their distant ancestors, which once lived on land. Turtles are reptiles, a group of animals more usually associated with hot, dry habitats. However, they are not the only reptiles to have made the transition to life in the ocean. The world's tropical waters are also home to several dozen species of sea snakes, some of which also periodically come ashore to lay their eggs. More than half of the world's sea snakes spend every moment of their lives at sea, however, giving birth to live young which can swim from the second they are born.

Coastal habitats are harsh places for animals to live but they draw people in huge numbers. For most of us, this is where our experience of the sea begins and ends.

Above: *Many seaweeds live between the tides and are regularly exposed to the air. They stay moist by retaining seawater in their tissues, soaked up and held in by absorbent molecules of algin.*

Below: *Many seabirds nest on coastal cliffs. Puffins dig burrows on the tops of cliffs in which to lay their eggs but often rest, as here, on wide ledges and spurs of rock.*

Rocky Shores

Shoreline habitats in general are difficult places for animals to live, but rocky coastlines are particularly challenging. Unlike sandy and muddy shores, which tend to slope gently into the sea, rocky shores are often steep or even vertical where they meet the water. This causes problems because waves hitting them often impact with great force. In order to survive here and not be washed away, it is vital for animals to have a very good grip on the rock.

One creature famous for its grip is the limpet. A mollusc from the same family as slugs and snails, it feeds, when the tide is in, on algae growing on the rocks, scraping away at it with microscopic, horny teeth. Like their land-living cousins, limpets are slow movers, travelling by means of a single, muscular foot. It is this that they use to maintain their hold on the rock against the buffeting of the waves. As the tide drops, they each head back to a particular favourite spot, following the trails of slime they left earlier. Once they reach these spots, they pull themselves hard against the rock forming a watertight seal, which keeps their soft bodies safe when the tide is out. The position each limpet adopts before pulling itself down is very precise and over time grooves are worn into the rock which exactly match the individual shapes of their shells. Even when they are on the move, limpets are very sensitive to being exposed to the air and pull themselves tight against the rock in-between waves. This reaction helps to make them less vulnerable to predatory birds such as oystercatchers, which patrol the waterline in search of molluscs on which to feed.

Limpets may have a strong grip but barnacles hold on even more tightly. Crustaceans rather than molluscs, they literally cement them-

selves to the rock. Like many rocky shore dwellers, barnacles are filter feeders, sifting out tiny particles of food that wash over them with the waves. They do this by means of their feathery legs, which have no loco-motive function at all. As adults, barnacles spend their whole lives fixed to one spot, waiting for their food to come to them. Before that, however, they live as microscopic larvae, drifting along as part of the plankton. They only change into adults when they settle on a solid surface. This is usually rock, but may be the skin of a whale or the hull of a ship.

Other rocky shore filter feeders include mussels, which connect themselves to the rock with tough threads. These are produced when, as larvae, they first settle out of the plankton. The threads are formed from a sticky liquid which turns solid when it comes into contact with water.

Holding on to the rocks may prevent mussels from being washed away by the waves but it does not protect them from predators. When the tide is out, they are exposed to attack from anything capable of smashing through their shells. Oystercatchers specialize in doing this, hammering away at mussels with their powerful bills. If the slightest gap appears between the paired shells, they wedge their bills in and lever them open. Failing that, they continue to bludgeon away until they break through.

Opposite: *When the tide goes out rock pools remain like little oases. Starfish leave these when the sea returns, but sea anemones stay put, their rubbery bodies firmly attached to the rock.*

Above: *Mussels are among the most common shellfish to be found on rocky shores. When the tide is out they keep their paired shells firmly shut. The open shells here are empty, victims of oystercatchers.*

Above right: *Turnstones are a common sight on rocky shores in Europe and North America. These birds feed on small creatures which they find beneath pebbles and seaweed.*

Page 12: *A marine iguana basks between dives for seaweed. These prehistoric-looking reptiles are endemic to the Galápagos Islands and found nowhere else in the world.*

Page 13: *Waves sweep up Laguna Beach, California. As well as being rugged, rocky shores can be incredibly beautiful.*

A close relative of the mussels, called the common piddock, has evolved a way to avoid the attentions of oystercatchers and other shore-dwelling birds. It burrows into the rock itself, excavating a chamber with the sharp edges of its hinged shells. As it grows, it continually rasps away with its shells so that the chamber grows with it. The entrance hole, however, remains the same size – big enough for the piddock to extend through the flexible tube of its siphon, which it uses to suck in water and the tiny particles of food it contains, but not big enough for the animal itself to escape, or be pulled out.

Most filter feeders live sedentary lives, waiting for their meals to come to them, but carnivores tend to be more mobile. Sea anemones, however, are an exception to this rule. They hunt on rocky shores while remaining in one spot.

Sea anemones are members of the same group of animals as jellyfish and they hunt in a similar way. They catch their food by using long, stinging tentacles. Whenever a fish, prawn or other small creatures touches one of these it finds itself being impaled by many microscopic poison darts, which quickly paralyse it. The sea anemone then wraps its tentacles around its hapless victim and pulls it towards the mouth in the centre of its body. Sea anemones themselves are sometimes attacked by larger fish and they can pull their tentacles into the muscular bases of their bodies to protect them. They also do this to conserve water and prevent themselves drying out if they find themselves exposed at low tide.

The sea anemones and shellfish of rocky shores either live fixed to the spot or move so slowly that they are often caught out by the falling tide.

Many other creatures, however, travel with the tide so that they always remain underwater. Shore crabs and hermit crabs feed on dead and decaying matter that they find amongst the seaweed, and are able to cling on with their jointed legs to prevent themselves being washed away by the surf. Shore crabs have a tough carapace, which protects them from most predators. Hermit crabs have softer bodies but shelter within the empty shells of dead molluscs, carrying them around on their backs wherever they go.

Many fish of rocky shores are also able to hold on and prevent themselves being swept away by the crashing waves. The aptly named two-spotted clingfish of European coasts is just one example. It forms a sucker disc on its belly with its two pelvic fins which sticks it to the rock.

Above the waterline on rocky shores life is much less abundant than it is below. Few creatures live here all year round, the exceptions in most parts of the world being some seals and wading birds. Around Britain and the east coast of Canada, grey seals can often be seen hauled out on rocky shores. Although they feed on fish and other free-swimming creatures in the water, they spend a lot of time on the shores themselves at rest, even when they do not have pups.

Rocky-shore birds include oystercatchers and turnstones. Various species of these birds inhabit different parts of the world, but wherever they are found, they behave in a similar way. Oystercatchers, as already

Opposite: *Seaweeds are more common on rocky shores than anywhere else. Strong yet flexible, they move with the water rather than resisting its force. Seaweeds are attached to the rocks by structures called holdfasts, which prevent them from being washed away.*

Below: *A Sally Lightfoot crab scuttles across a Galápagos shore. Many crabs are almost as at home out of the sea as in it, scavenging for food both above and below the waterline.*

mentioned, specialize in eating mussels – in fact, they would be better named 'musselcatchers,' as they rarely eat oysters at all. Turnstones are much more accurately named. They find their food – small crabs and other tiny animals – by flipping over pebbles and seaweed.

There is one part of the world that has rocky-shore creatures like those of nowhere else – the Galápagos Islands. Isolated from the rest of the world by a vast expanse of sea, its strange fauna famously inspired Charles Darwin to develop his theory of evolution through natural selection. The Galápagos Islands are home to the world's only seagoing lizard, the marine iguana. This prehistoric-looking animal feeds entirely on seaweed, which it grazes from the islands' rocky shores. In some places, the rocks are crowded with marine iguanas, jostling for space as they feed or stand stock-still soaking up the sun. Females and young males graze on the rocks as the tide recedes but larger males actually dive beneath the surface in search of food. Like all reptiles, their body temperatures rise and fall with those of their surroundings so they rarely stay underwater for long, instead returning to the rocks to bask before they become too cold and sluggish.

Marine iguanas share the rocks with flightless cormorants, sea birds that are also found nowhere else on Earth. The cormorants dive in the waters around the islands for fish and come out on to the shore to dry themselves in the sun.

Although flightless cormorants are unique to the Galápagos Islands, they have flying relatives living along shores in most parts of the world. Like flightless cormorants, they too stand in the sun with their wings outstretched to dry out their feathers. Many of them also share the flightless cormorant's predilection for nesting on rocky shores.

Cormorants tend to nest at the base of cliffs on rocky coasts, close to the water. Being large birds and clumsy fliers, they are not well suited to nesting on the ledges above.

However, many other birds do make use of these high-rise sites. In spring and summer, above the cormorants and their relatives the shags, a whole range of sea birds lay their eggs. Auks such as guillemots and razorbills crowd the wider ledges, laying their eggs on the bare rock. The eggs of these species are pointed at one end so that they tend to roll around in circles if knocked, to prevent them falling off. The more precarious sites are taken by fulmars and gulls such as kittiwakes. These birds are more agile in the air, enabling them to land where auks cannot.

Gannets also nest on rocky shores, although the sites they choose tend to be either large cliff ledges or the tops of stacks or islands. Like guillemots, razorbills and kittiwakes, they nest close together, but they are large birds and each pair needs more space.

Puffins dig burrows in the grass at the tops of cliffs. Like the other birds that nest on these shores they make several trips out to sea every day in order to catch enough food for their chicks.

Previous pages: *A gannet sits on its nest, one of hundreds in a busy colony. Gannets are large birds that dive from the air to catch fish, folding back their wings just before impact to enter the water like missiles.*

Following pages: *Seagulls are so ubiquitous on shorelines that we often fail to notice them. Their success is due largely to their adaptability. Most species scavenge as much as they hunt and will feed happily on almost anything.*

Left: *Grey seals rest on rocks just offshore. The grey seal is found only in the shallow coastal waters of the North Atlantic Ocean. Almost two thirds of the world's population lives around the British Isles.*

Above: *Rocky shores provide havens for nesting sea birds, most of which spend the rest of their lives far out at sea. In this picture, guillemots and kittiwakes crowd on to cliff ledges around the Farne Islands, just off the coast of Northumberland.*

Top: Hermit crabs are often encountered on rocky shores. These little crustaceans hide their bodies inside discarded sea snails' shells, which they carry around with them everywhere they go.

Above: Although sea anemones look like flowers, they are actually closely related to jellyfish. Like them, they have stinging tentacles, which they use to catch prey, such as small fish, marine worms and crustaceans.

Left: Marine iguanas seem to grow from the rocks they inhabit. Like their inland cousins, these lizards are cold-blooded and have to bask in the sun to warm up.

Sandy shores

I f rocky shores are barren, sandy shores are even more so. By their nature, they are constantly shifting and so provide nothing for seaweed to cling to. Most creatures that live on sandy beaches are scavengers, relying almost entirely on what the sea washes up. Gulls wander the shoreline looking for scraps but often there are no other large animals to be seen.

Anyone who has walked along the shoreline on a sandy beach will be familiar with one of the few specialists of this habitat, the sandhopper. Sandhoppers are crustaceans closely related to freshwater shrimps and they live almost entirely on rotting seaweed. Various species live on sandy beaches in different parts of the world but they all look very similar and behave in a similar way. The easiest way to see them, if they are not already visible, is to lift up a piece of seaweed. With their cover gone, the sandhoppers beneath leap around in all directions, sometimes flying more than two feet (61cm) in the air. These little creatures, no more than half an inch (1.27cm) long, propel themselves with a powerful flick of the tail, something their aquatic cousins do when they need to shoot quickly through the water.

Sea slaters, like sandhoppers, are crustaceans that live near the high-tide mark on sandy beaches and scavenge dead matter. Although they too are common worldwide, they are less often seen as they tend to be nocturnal, spending the day hidden away in crevices or beneath driftwood. Sea slaters are closely related to woodlice, or sow bugs, and look like giant versions of them, sometimes reaching an inch (2.54cm) in length.

The dry sand at the tops of beaches is almost barren, but, wherever water penetrates, life survives. Tiny nematode worms swim between the

grains, hoovering up detritus and single-celled algae. Farther down, where the sand is regularly covered by water, larger invertebrates can be found. Bivalve molluscs, such as cockles and tellins, hide among the grains unseen. When the tide is out they clamp their paired shells shut, but they open them again whenever they are covered by water. They live by sucking water into their bodies through tube-shaped siphons, which they stick up just above the surface of the sand, then filtering out the the plankton and other tiny particles of food it contains.

Where the sand never dries, other creatures can be found. Bristle worms live here, buried, even when the tide is in, apart from the feeding tentacles which give them their name. Just beyond the water's edge, starfish comb the sediment for carrion and flattened sea urchins called sand dollars trap particles of food with the sticky mucus between their short spines. There are even fish, although they tend to be fairly few and scattered. In European waters this habitat is favoured by the lesser weaver, which lies burrowed in the sand, waiting for prey. Like most fish that live along sandy shores it is well camouflaged, with the skin on its upper side a perfect match for the sand in which it hides.

Page 26: *A soldier crab patrols its patch of beach on a Pacific island. Soldier crabs feed on microscopic organisms, which they filter out from the wet sand at the water's edge.*

Page 27: *Gentle waves lap a deserted sand beach on the north shore of Hawaii. The fine, almost white sand of such tropical beaches is made up largely of delicate, crushed particles of coral from the reefs just offshore.*

Below: *A painted ghost crab emerges from its burrow on a sandy shore in Chile. Ghost crabs make their burrows above the high-tide line but forage at the edge of the surf.*

In warmer waters, garden eels also live burrowed in the sands just off-shore. These little fish feed on planktonic animals, which they snap from the water as the tides move over them. They live communally, each spaced a little apart, and could be mistaken for seagrass were it not for their habit of disappearing into their burrows when approached.

Small fish burrow or bury themselves to stay out of sight of predators, but this tactic only serves to protect them from larger fish that hunt by sight alone. Rays, which may also be found in the shallows just off sandy beaches, have an extra sense at their disposal to expose hidden prey. Like their relatives the sharks, they can detect the tiny electric pulses given off by muscle activity and so can effectively 'see' fish even when they are completely covered by sand.

The waters that lap sandy shores are far from rich but most of the time they are positively teeming with life compared with the beaches themselves. All this changes when the visitors arrive, however. Many beaches are seen by some marine creatures as ideal places to breed.

Every spring, the Atlantic coast of North America is invaded by horse-shoe crabs, which gather in their thousands on some sandy beaches. These alien-looking creatures are not true crabs at all but relics of an ancient and once widespread group of marine invertebrates distantly related to spiders. They spend most of the year just offshore, scouring the sea floor for burrowing worms and other small prey but leave the water en masse to spawn and lay their eggs near the high-tide line. Here, the eggs develop and hatch out of reach of seagoing predators. The larvae enter the sea weeks later, climbing up through the grains and swimming out with the next receding high tide.

Above: *Garden eels feed on tiny planktonic creatures, which they snap from the water as currents wash them by. These timid fish dig burrows in the sand just off beaches, disappearing into them at the slightest hint of danger.*

Below: *Sandhoppers live in and feed on rotting seaweed, which builds up on sandy beaches around the high tide mark. Their name comes from their tendency to fire themselves high into the air if disturbed, taking off with a powerful flick of the tail.*

Turtles also take advantage of the relative safety of sandy beaches. They are forced to leave the sea because their eggs cannot develop in water and they choose sandy beaches because they are the easiest to excavate. Different species of turtles prefer different beaches and they return to the same ones unerringly year after year.

Having mated at sea, female turtles head towards their favoured beaches and gather offshore. Most wait until until sunset to haul themselves out, as their freshly laid eggs are less vulnerable at night to predators, particularly birds. Slowly and laboriously, each turtle digs a hole with her flippers in which to lay her eggs. By dawn, most have finished, buried their clutches and returned to the sea. The young turtles hatch out weeks later, most at the same time, and make a dash for the sea.

Many seals and sea lions choose sandy beaches to both mate and have their young. Northern elephant seals are typical. The first to arrive are the adult males, who battle for territory on the offshore island beaches of California and Mexico. The victors stake their claim to a patch of sand and the defeated are driven back into the sea. When the much smaller females arrive, the males gather them into harems, which they defend from neighbouring rivals The males mate with receptive females and already pregnant females pup. Soon after giving birth, they too are mated, most to return pregnant to the same beaches the following year.

Left: *The world's five species of sea turtle rely on sandy shores as places to lay their eggs. Here a green turtle covers her eggs after laying them in the sand on Ascension Island in the Atlantic Ocean.*

Above: *Most baby turtles hatch at night, to avoid predators, but a few are still making their way down to the sea at dawn. Those females that survive to adulthood will eventually return to the beach where they hatched to lay their own eggs.*

Right: Southern elephant seals haul out on beaches to pup. Males fight for dominance over certain areas of the beach and the right to mate with any females that settle there. The southern elephant seal is the world's largest seal, with males growing up to 13 feet (4m) long and weighing as much as 2 tons/tonnes.

Above: The sun sets over Indian Beach at the edge of Ecola State Park, Oregon, USA. Although beaches may seem permanent, they are slowly but almost continuously on the move, growing in some places and disappearing in others as the never-ending force of the waves shifts their sands along the coast.

Left: Stingrays are perfectly designed for life on the seabed, with flattened bodies that hug the bottom. These fish, related to sharks, move by undulating their muscular pectoral wings and feed on crustaceans and other creatures that live or hide themselves in the sand. Stingrays do not see their prey but rather find it by means of smell and electroreception, picking up the tiny electrical currents given off by the muscles of buried animals.

Above: Stingrays live in the world's tropical and subtropical waters, and tend to be concentrated in greatest numbers near to coasts. There are around 70 different species altogether. This one is swimming in the waters lapping a beach in the Maldives. The poisonous sting that gives these fish their name is located on the upper part of the tail. It is only used for defence as a last resort: stingrays are generally placid and avoid danger rather than confronting it.

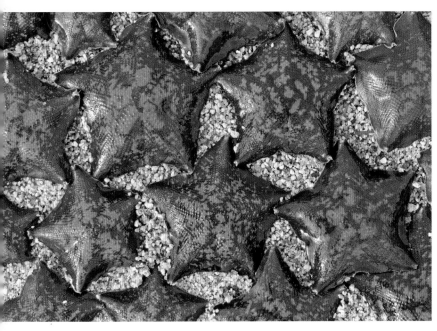

Top: Seagulls do a good job of keeping beaches clean, snapping up anything edible that washes on to shore, including the occasional fish.

Above: Young starfish are briefly exposed by the falling tide. They will be vulnerable to predators until the next tide covers them.

Right: Starfish are not true fish at all but members of another group of animals called the echinoderms. Most species feed on shellfish, which they find in the sand.

Estuaries and mud flats

Estuaries and mud flats form where rivers meet the sea. They are created from the sediment in rivers that is washed off the land and deposited at their mouths. Estuaries and mud flats are the most productive of all coastal habitats, the rich ooze supporting a huge abundance of life, much of it buried and unseen. Tiny algae thrive on the surface of the sediment and in the nutrient-rich waters that wash over it, supporting worms and other animals, which also feed on organic detritus and rotting matter held within the mud itself. These in turn support fish and wading birds.

The abundance of life found in estuaries is doubled by the fact that both freshwater and saltwater creatures can live here. Fresh water is continually brought in by the rivers that feed estuaries, while salt water flows upstream twice daily with the incoming tides. Fresh water, being less dense than brine, tends to float on the top for some distance before the two mingle together. The opposing flows of the river and incoming tide slow the overall downstream movement of water, causing the suspended sediment to be deposited.

Estuaries are very dynamic environments that change a great deal with the tides. When the tide is in and the mud flats are covered, the many filter-feeding animals that live in the sediment are able to feed. Cockles, furrow shells, tellins and other bivalve molluscs extend their siphons up through the sediment and sieve the water for plankton. Predatory ragworms stick their heads from their burrows to grab shrimps and other small animal prey, while lugworms continue to eat their way through the mud just as they do when the tide is out, digesting the organic matter and expelling the rest.

Fish also appear over the mud flats at high tide to feed on the many invertebrates crawling around or peeking out of their burrows. Unable to see far in the muddy waters, many have evolved other ways of communicating. Drums, grunts and croakers, for example, all communicate by sound. As well as estuary specialists, the rising tide brings in marine fish such as flounders and grey mullet. These are, in turn, hunted by animals more often associated with inland waters than the sea, such as river otters and herons.

When the tide falls and the mud flats are exposed, a different shift of creatures moves in. Crabs scurry about the surface, providing food for birds such as shelducks and flocks of waders which quickly appear.

The sheer numbers of wading birds seen in estuaries are a testament to the hidden abundance of life in the mud. All of them feed on the worms, shellfish and other small creatures that live there. Food is so thickly spread that all they have to do is probe their bills in and snap up anything they touch. Different species of waders specialize in catching different prey. Those with the longest bills, such as curlews and godwits, are able to dig down for ragworms, lugworms and other deep burrowers, while those with shorter bills probe for the small crustaceans and shellfish that live near the top.

Page 38: A West Indian manatee cruises through shallow water at a river mouth.

Page 39: Estuaries form where rivers meet the sea. The sudden mixing of fresh and salt water causes sediment to sink to the bottom, creating extensive mudflats.

Below: An American avocet sifts through the water overlying estuary mud. Avocets feed on tiny creatures, which they snap from the water with the upturned ends of their bills, unlike most waders, which probe for their food in the mud.

Left: *Ragworms inhabit estuaries in their millions. Most species are hunters, grabbing prey from the water when the tide is in. When the water recedes, they themselves become prey to curlews and other long-billed wading birds. Other, shorter-billed waders are unable to reach them, hidden at the bottoms of their burrows.*

Below: *Although mudflats often look lifeless, they are in fact teeming with creatures, most of which lie hidden just beneath the surface. Per unit area, estuarine mudflats are among the most productive habitats on Earth, generating more organic matter than grasslands, forests or agricultural land.*

Many wading bird species form huge flocks which comb the freshly exposed mudflats in jittery crowds, ready to take flight at the slightest hint of danger. Bringing up the rear behind these birds at the water's edge are other waders, which prefer to forage in pairs or alone. These birds, which tend to have relatively short bills, include such species as the ringed plover. Rather than probing the mud for prey, they tend to search more widely and examine the surface, snapping up any small animals that they find there.

Most wading birds feed by catching individual animals but flamingoes sift the water and swallow dozens of tiny animal prey at a time. They are among the largest birds found in estuaries and are restricted mainly to the world's tropical and subtropical regions. In more temperate regions, avocets feed on similar, slightly larger prey. Unlike flamingoes, they catch the creatures they eat individually, sweeping the upturned ends of their bills through the water and snapping them shut as soon as they touch anything.

Not all birds in estuaries feed by scouring the mud or wading. The skimmer catches its meals while flying along. Skimmers are unusual in having bills with the lower mandible longer than the upper. This is an adaptation to the way they feed. As the name suggests, skimmers fly very low over the water and they drag the long lower halves of their bills through the surface as they go. Small fish at the surface are scooped up, grabbed and swallowed while the bird is still on the wing. After making one pass over an area of water, a skimmer turns in the air and trawls back across in the other direction.

Skimmers have a unique way of feeding but they are far from the only birds that frequent estuaries to hunt fish. Terns are also attracted to hunt the shoals of small fish often found in these waters. Rather than skimming, they dive on their prey from above.

In late summer and fall, the estuaries of the Northern Hemisphere play host to an incredible migration. Huge shoals of salmon arrive to begin the last leg of an annual struggle to reach their breeding grounds. Salmon hatch and spend their early lives upriver but travel downstream as they become adults then spending years of life at sea. When they finally reach breeding size and condition they return to the rivers of their birth to spawn. How they navigate across the ocean remains a mystery, but what is known is that they recognize the chemical 'fingerprint' of their home river and are drawn towards it as they taste it mixed with the sea water along the coast. Every river has a slightly different fingerprint, made up of traces of the many minerals it washes over in its journey to the sea. This fingerprint becomes imprinted on the young salmon's memory and stays with it all its life.

As salmon near the estuaries of their home rivers, the distinctive flavour in the surrounding sea becomes stronger and they are drawn ever more frantically in. On certain days the river mouths become thick with

their wriggling bodies, providing a bonanza for predatory animals, birds and anglers alike.

A few large mammals specialize in living in estuaries. Among them are two species of sea cow, the West Indian and the West African manatees. These placid, herbivorous creatures may each weigh well over a ton/tonne. They survive entirely on water plants, which they graze in peace, having no natural predators. As its name suggests, the West Indian manatee is most common around the shores of the Caribbean Sea, but it also occurs on the Atlantic coast of southern Florida. The West African manatee can be found in estuaries and river basins from Senegal to Angola, as well as in sheltered bays along the coast.

A few species of dolphin also inhabit estuaries. Able to communicate with sound and to find food using echolocation, they have no difficulty at all surviving in the muddy waters around river mouths. The little-known Franciscana is common in the La Plata estuary, which divides Uruguay from Argentina, and also occurs in shallow coastal waters and other estuaries as far north as Brazil. Around the Indo-Pacific, the Irrawaddy dolphin favours similar habitats, although it is also found living in the fresh water of rivers farther upstream. Other dolphins known to inhabit estuaries include Hector's dolphin from New Zealand and the Indo-Pacific humpbacked dolphin. Many other species visit estuaries but tend more often to be found in clearer waters farther offshore.

Previous pages: Western sandpipers rest on an exposed bank at high tide in Alaska. Like most waders, they feed as the tide goes out, following the retreating edge of the water to catch small creatures that find themselves suddenly exposed.

Above: Cockles are among the many bivalve shellfish that live in estuary mud.

Right: Flamingoes sift algae and tiny animals from the water using their uniquely-shaped beaks, which are lined with rows of horny plates.

Left: The Irrawaddy dolphin is named after a river in Myanmar (Burma) but inhabits large rivers, estuaries and coastal waters from eastern India to Indonesia and Vietnam. It seems equally at home in fresh or salt water. Some individuals spend their whole lives in rivers while others never enter them, instead patrolling coastal waters next to the shore.

Above: The peacock flounder is one of the world's more colourful flatfish. Most of its relatives are cryptically camouflaged and some can even change colour to match the sea floor on which they lie. As hatchlings, flounders swim in open water and look much like other fish. As they grow older their bodies change, twisting so that both eyes end up on the same 'upper' side.

Previous pages: *A West Indian manatee swims with her calf. Manatees feed on seaweed and other marine vegetation. Together with their relative the dugong, which inhabits coastal waters around Indonesia and Australia, they make up a group known as sea cows, the world's only herbivorous marine mammals.*

Above: *Crab plovers scour dry mudflats, covered only by the highest tides. Most plovers have relatively short bills for wading birds, reflecting their diets, which are made up mainly of invertebrates found on the surface rather than in the mud itself.*

Mangrove forests

Mangroves are the only trees that can survive in salt water. In the tropics and subtropics they fringe many parts of the coast in dense forests, so tangled that they are impenetrable except where divided by inlets, river channels and creeks.

Mangroves play an important role in protecting coastlines from erosion and creating new land. Sediment quickly settles around their networks of aerial roots, which also deaden and dissipate the energy of waves lapping the shore. These roots not only prop the trees up but take in oxygen, when the tide is out, through pores in their surface. Some species have prop roots which stick out from their stems and subdivide before they reach the mud. Others have roots that snake out beneath the mud like those of normal trees but send up vertical pillars every so often which break through the mud to take in air.

Mangroves are most common at the mouths of rivers, taking over deltas and covering estuarine mud flats, which, in colder climes, might be devoid of plants. However, they are also found along muddy shores that are far from rivers, including those of many islands. Like coconut palms, they produce seeds that float and can travel long distances at sea. These may colonize new areas far from their parents. On the other hand, mangrove seeds may grow into new plants right next to the trees that produced them. It all depends on whether the tide is in or out when they fall. Some species have seeds that are spear shaped with heavy, pointed tips. These actually germinate while still attached to their parents and stick firmly in the mud when it is not covered by water.

Excess salt is deadly to plants and would kill mangroves if they had not evolved methods to cope with it. Some get rid of salt by concentrat-

ing it in their older leaves, which are then shed, to be replaced by new ones. Others have glands on the leaves which excrete a salt solution far more concentrated than sea water.

The saltiness of mangrove leaves makes them inedible to most creatures, but there is one animal that eats almost nothing else – the proboscis monkey. This strange looking primate inhabits the mangrove forests of Borneo and is entirely vegetarian, eating mangrove shoots and seeds as well as leaves. As befits its habitat, it is an extremely accomplished swimmer, with partially webbed back feet. There are records of proboscis monkeys being picked up alive by fishing boats more than a mile (1.6km) out at sea.

Although a few creatures live in the branches of mangrove forests, the vast majority inhabit the mud and water beneath. Crustaceans are particularly numerous here, with different species inhabiting different zones. On the landward side, where only the highest tides reach, mud lobsters are common. These shy but quite large crustaceans are nocturnal, spending the day in deep burrows with their entrances plugged up with mud. As night falls, they emerge to feed, carefully removing the organic matter from the mud around their burrows and piling up the waste material in volcano-shaped mounds. Alongside the mud lobsters live several types of large burrowing crabs. These feed on fallen mangrove leaves. When they are not feeding, they gather leaf litter and pull it down into their burrows. Some of this is eaten later but the rest rots down, enriching the mangrove mud.

Page 52: Mudskippers spend much of their time out of water. As well as holding water over their gills, they can absorb oxygen from the air through their skin.

Page 53: Mangroves are the only trees able to survive with their roots in seawater. This ability has enabled them to colonize huge areas of shoreline in the tropics.

Below: The mangrove jack lives along the northern shores of Australia, where it is a common fish, well known to anglers. It also occurs along coasts throughout the Indian Ocean and in the South Pacific as far east as Samoa. Like many tropical fish, the mangrove jack spends its younger years living among the sheltering tangles of mangrove tree roots. When it reaches adulthood, it moves to deeper waters but remains near the coast.

Nearer the low-tide mark, fiddler crabs are the dominant crustaceans. When the tide is out they pick through the mud for any organic matter the waters may have left behind. Female fiddler crabs use both sets of pincers to feed but the males are at something of a disadvantage. They have one small set of pincers, like those of the females, which are perfect for searching for food. The other set, however, is enormous and completely useless for feeding. In some species, it may be as heavy as the rest of the crab's body. This set is used for display and fighting. Male fiddlers wave their giant claws to intimidate rivals and attract females to mate. They also use them to grapple other males and fight them. In some individuals the left claw is the outsized one, while in others it is the right.

The mud in mangrove forests is regularly inundated and exposed by the tides. Most fish that live here move in and out with the water. Young fish, in particular, find shelter among the tangled roots, out of reach of many larger fish that predate them in more open waters. Even here though, small fish are not completely safe. Birds such as night herons hunt them instead, waiting motionless on the trees' prop roots for prey to pass below. Kingfishers are also quite common in mangrove forests. In the mangrove forests of Africa and Asia the pied kingfisher is one of the most abundant birds. This agile bird may hunt by diving from a conven-

Above: Fiddler crabs are a common sight in mangrove swamps around Africa, Asia and the eastern Pacific. Close relatives of ghost crabs, they feed on particles they find in the mud. Male fiddler crabs have one hugely enlarged claw, which they use to fight rival males and display to females. In some males the left claw is enlarged, while in others it is the right.

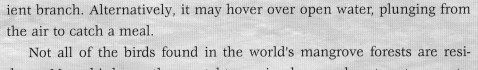

ient branch. Alternatively, it may hover over open water, plunging from the air to catch a meal.

Not all of the birds found in the world's mangrove forests are residents. Many birds use the coastal trees simply as a place to set up nests. Boobies are seafarers closely related to gannets that often travel quite long distances to find shoals of fish out in the ocean. Like all birds however, they must return to land to breed and the branches of mangrove forests provide perfect platforms for their colonies. Frigate birds also gather to nest in these trees. It is the males which build the nests and attract the females to mate, inflating their scarlet throat sacs like balloons to advertise their eligibility. Frigate birds are sometimes called aerial pirates and it is a good description. They get their food by stealing it from other fish-eating sea birds, harassing them in flight until they drop or regurgitate their catch.

Around the Bay of Bengal and the Indo-Pacific without doubt the most feared predator of the mangrove forests is the saltwater crocodile. This prehistoric-looking monster is the world's largest living reptile, growing to 20 feet (6m) long and often weighing well over a ton/tonne. Saltwater crocodiles are fearless and aggressive hunters which count human beings on their list of prey. As the name suggests, they are just as at home in the sea as they are in fresh or brackish water, and they are accomplished ocean travellers, often swimming long distances to find new islands and prey.

Left: *Frigate birds are ocean wanderers that harry other birds to steal their prey. At certain times of the year they gather to breed, often using mangrove trees as nesting platforms. Only the males have the red neck pouch, which they inflate to attract females.*

Above: *The stilt roots of a mangrove tree give it support and also help it to take up oxygen from the air. Normal trees absorb oxygen from the air pockets in the soil around their roots, but for mangroves, which live in water, this is not an option.*

Saltwater crocodiles are amphibious creatures, spending time both in and out of water. While this is not unusual among reptiles it is not a trait one normally associates with fish. Mudskippers, however, are also just as at home out of water as in it. These little fish live in mangrove forests throughout Africa, Asia and the Indo-Pacific and are surprisingly common almost wherever they are found. Like all fish, mudskippers have gills which they use to extract oxygen from water but, unusually, they can also absorb oxygen from the air through their skin. While they cannot stay on land indefinitely, this is where they find their food. Some species are carnivorous, hunting crabs, insects and, occasionally, other mudskippers. Others feed on algae and other organic matter in the mud.

Different species of mudskippers inhabit different levels on the shore but none stray far above the high-tide mark. Although they can take oxygen from the air, they still largely rely on their gills, which they keep covered with water. When they are on land they keep the entrances to their gill chambers shut to hold water in, but every so often they have to return to the sea or pools that they dig to replenish their supplies.

Mudskippers have other adaptations to living out of water as well as the obvious ones regarding breathing. Their pectoral fins, for example, have muscular bases and act almost like legs, propelling them over the mud. Some species can even use these fins to climb up mangrove roots in order to catch food.

Mudskippers' eyes are positioned like turrets on top of their heads. This gives them a 360 degree view of the world around them, so that they can easily spot danger from behind or from the air. It also enables them to see what is going on above the waterline when their bodies are submerged. Interestingly, their eyes are divided horizontally, with the top halves providing colour vision and the bottom halves black and white.

Like fiddler crabs, mudskippers dig burrows into which they retreat when the tide returns. These also provide useful bolt holes to escape predators when the tide is out.

Left: Although mudskippers can spend long periods in the open air, they must periodically immerse themselves to replace the water covering their gills.

Right: Saltwater crocodiles are ferocious and aggressive predators, with no fear of humans. They are thought to kill well over 1000 people across their range every year, many times more than all of the world's sharks put together.

Left: *Some mangrove trees have seeds with weighted, spiked ends. If the tide is out when these drop, they stick into the mud and begin to germinate straight away. If the tide is in, the seeds bob back up to the surface and are carried away by the currents to be washed up and germinate elsewhere.*

Above: *Small fish hide among mangrove roots, which they use to shield themselves from larger predators. Although mangroves offer protection from swimming predators, they provide perches for fish-eating birds, such as kingfishers and herons, which may attack suddenly and without warning from above.*

Above: Mangrove forests help to stabilize shorelines and build new land, holding together mud and other sediments, which would otherwise be quickly washed away by the flowing tides. As well as providing a habitat for marine life, they also attract birds and arboreal animals, such as monkeys.

Left: Herons and other predatory birds will often sit among mangroves looking into the water below for the small fish and crustaceans on which they feed.

Opposite: Sea snakes are common in the waters around mangrove swamps. Some species, such as this one, the banded sea krait, lay their eggs on beaches. Others, however, give birth to live young and never leave the sea.

Chapter 2
Coastal Waters

Rich Pickings

The waters around the world's coasts are the richest in the sea. A constant stream of nutrients pours into them, washed off the land, while upwelling currents bring more organic matter and minerals up from the deep. Most coastal waters are relatively shallow, lying over continental shelf. This stretches out for miles like a gently sloping collar around the world's major land masses, before ending abruptly and plummeting to the great depths of the open ocean's dark abyssal plain.

Coastal waters closest to shore are the richest in life because here light is able to penetrate to the bottom. Plants such as eelgrass and algae such as kelp and other seaweeds flourish, harnessing the light of the sun to photosynthesize and generate food. They in turn support great populations of animals.

Tropical corals also need light to survive. Although their rocky reefs look like gardens, they are created by animals, colonies of tiny polyps related to jellyfish and sea anemones. The polyps each house single-celled algae within their body tissues and these require sunlight in order to produce the sugars on which their polyp hosts partly rely. Coral reefs, like kelp forests and eelgrass beds, create distinct habitats containing numerous niches, each of which has its own unique community of animal life.

Even where they are too deep for light to reach the bottom, coastal waters tend to be richer than those anywhere else. The reason for this is their abundant supplies of new nutrients, which are constantly mixed at the surface by the actions of currents and waves. These nutrients are utilized by phytoplankton – microscopic algae and other tiny photosynthesizing organisms that live in the upper layers of the sea. Their drifting clouds are fed on by zooplankton and larger animals such as fish, which in turn support sea birds and other ocean predators.

Right: To most of us, coastal waters are the most familiar parts of the ocean, the thin line that separates the land from the depths beyond.

Kelp forests

People often call coral reefs the rain forests of the sea. By the same analogy, kelp forests are the ocean's taiga. Like the coniferous trees that make up that habitat on land, kelp thrive in cold conditions and grow in uniform abundance. The larger forests are found in waters with temperatures no higher than 68°F (20°C), extending right up to the edges of the Arctic and Antarctic Circles.

Kelp are gigantic seaweeds and, like most of their smaller relatives, they require firm foundations on which to attach themselves. For this reason, they are only found around rocky coastlines where the seabed is solid or formed from large boulders. They anchor themselves with structures known as holdfasts. These look like the root bundles of plants (kelp are algae, members of a related but distinct kingdom) but unlike them play no part in absorbing water or nutrients. Their sole purpose is to grow into cracks and crevices, filling them so that the kelp itself cannot be dragged away and washed ashore or swept out to sea.

Above the holdfast is a long, rope-like but flexible stem called a stipe. This is immensely strong and has to be in order to withstand the buffeting of storm-driven waves. Growing from the stipe or extending from its end, depending on the species, are great strap-like fronds packed with photosynthesizing pigment. In some kelp these can each stretch for dozens of feet. From holdfast to the tips of their most distant fronds, some kelp can measure nearly 200 feet (60m) long.

Kelp maintain their upright position in the water by means of large air-filled bladders. These ensure that the fronds receive as much light as possible, maximizing their ability to produce food. At low tide the fronds are often exposed to the air, but they never dry out. This is due to the

presence within them of large quantities of algin, a substance they produce which is incredibly water retentive.

Various types of kelp occur in different parts of the world but all of them possess the same basic structure. In most of the areas they are found they tend to form almost uniform submarine forests, dominated by a single species. In this way they again closely mirror the forests of taiga that divide broad-leafed forests from tundra on land.

Kelp adds a new and rare dimension to the underwater world, one of vertical structure. Creatures in kelp forests are not just restricted to the seabed or open water. They also live on and among the fronds themselves. Sea snails munch away at the surface of kelp fronds, along with small isopods, the marine equivalent of leaf-eating insects. These are kept in check by fish such as kelp bass and garibaldis, which, in turn, are eaten by diving birds, sea lions and seals.

The number of animals kelp forests support is surprisingly high. Different species prefer different zones. Señorita fish, for example, rarely venture far from the bottom, while topsmelt, as the name suggests, form small shoals in the canopy. Some creatures, such as the Pacific whitesided dolphin, regularly visit in search of food but do not live in the forests exclusively. Others are almost never found anywhere else.

Page 68: *Nudibranchs, better known as sea slugs, are among the more bizarre-looking inhabitants of the world's kelp forests.*

Page 69: *A garibaldi fish swims through kelp just off the coast of California.*

Opposite: *Kelp rely on sunlight to generate energy. Like trees on land they reach up towards the sun, but unlike trees are held up by gas floats rather than sturdy trunks.*

Below: *Kelp are giant seaweeds and, like most of their smaller relatives, live attached to the rock. Here, a grey seal lies among kelp holdfasts at low tide.*

One such resident specialist is the sea otter, which inhabits the kelp forests of the northern Pacific, ranging from the Kuril Islands and Russia's Kamchatka peninsula through Alaska and western Canada to the coast of California. Across much of its range it feeds almost exclusively on sea urchins and abalone, which thrive among kelp forests on the sea floor. After diving down to collect its prey, it finds a flat pebble before returning to the surface. Lying on its back, it balances the pebble on its chest and uses it as an anvil to smash open its prey and get at the soft flesh inside.

Where they occur, sea otters are important to the survival of kelp forests, protecting them by keeping the numbers of sea urchins down. These spiny invertebrates attack kelp holdfasts and can decimate the marine forests if left unchecked.

Unlike most marine mammals, sea otters have no layer of blubber to guard against the cold. Instead, they have an extremely luxuriant pelt, which traps a layer of air against the skin, keeping it both warm and dry. This pelt was almost the sea otter's undoing, as it was considered so desirable in the 18th and 19th centuries that the species was hunted close to extinction. Populations have yet to properly recover.

Sea otters are important predators of sea urchins but they are not the only creatures in kelp forests that eat them. Asteroid starfish, for example, also hunt sea urchins, as do horn sharks, undeterred by their defensive spines. Horn sharks are unusual in having flattened, plate-like teeth, evolved for crushing tough prey rather than slicing through flesh.

Many other creatures share the sea floor among the holdfasts. Among them are filter feeders such as fan worms, sponges and sea squirts. Spiny lobsters pick between the rocks for carrion, while octopuses and small sharks hunt. Off California, the leopard shark is a common visitor to the giant kelp forests, swimming in to scour the seabed for prey. Higher up in the water column, blue sharks patrol between the fronds.

The abundance of life in kelp forests reflects the many niches they offer. Many of the fish that live in them are found nowhere else, but others are simply drawn in from the surrounding waters by the prospect of prey. As well as food, kelp forests provide protection and somewhere to hide. It is much easier for fish to escape predators between the waving fronds than it would be out in open water.

Left: Kelp forests provide both food and protection for fish. Most feed on invertebrates and smaller fish rather than the kelp itself.

Right: Sea otters live along the Pacific coast of North America and are rarely found outside kelp forests. When asleep or at rest on the surface they wrap kelp fronds around their bodies to prevent themselves from drifting away.

Left: *With its bright orange coloration, the garibaldi fish is one of the most striking inhabitants of California's kelp forests. Adults maintain small home territories, which they guard from others of their kind.*

Above: *Unlike garibaldis, which tend to be solitary, señoritas are schooling fish. They feed on small invertebrate animals and sometimes pick the parasites off larger fish to eat.*

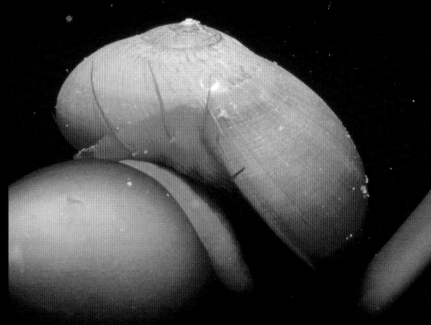

Top: Some sea snails feed on kelp. Like their land-living cousins, they scrape away at the surface of their food with a rasp-like 'tongue', or radula.

Above: Kelp bass are large fish that prey on smaller species. The spiky creatures behind this kelp bass are sea urchins.

Left: Pacific white-sided dolphins sometimes enter kelp forests to find prey.

Above: *Echinoderms are common on the rocks of the kelp forest floor. Here a sun star inches towards sea urchins off Canada's Vancouver Island.*

Right: *Sea urchins feed on kelp. In the past their numbers were controlled around north Pacific coasts by sea otters but decades of hunting decimated the population of these animals, their principal predators.*

Previous pages: *Kelp have long, flexible fronds of tissue that are the equivalent of leaves.*

Underwater pastures

Plants need sunlight to survive. Most also require oxygen from the air and their roots to be fed with fresh water. There is one group of flowering plants, however, that has adapted to life in the ocean. They are the seagrasses, or eelgrasses, as they are known in some places.

Seagrasses form beds in shallow waters along many coasts. They are true grasses, closely related to several species on land. Their beds form in calm areas with sandy or muddy bottoms, protected from the worst of the waves. In some places their swaying blades reach the surface. In others, where the water is especially clear, they may be found growing as much as 100 feet (30m) down.

Like other grasses, seagrasses anchor themselves with roots and spread partly by means of rhizomes – horizontal stems that grow through the sediment. They also produce simple flowers and seeds. Pollination, naturally, occurs underwater. Most land grasses use wind to carry their pollen from one flower to another, but in seagrasses these male sex cells are transported along with movements in the water.

Seagrasses occur in most parts of the world outside the polar regions and there are many different species. Most are relatively small, with blades just a few inches long, but some are giants. One which grows in the Sea of Japan has blades that reach over 12 feet (3.6m) in length. As with land plants, most tropical and subtropical seagrasses are evergreen, but in temperate areas, where the seasons are more pronounced, some species shed their leaves in preparation for winter.

Seagrass beds and meadows form their own unique habitats, providing sustenance and shelter for many different animals. A few are adapted specifically to live within them but most either visit or just spend part of

their lives there. Just as on land prairies may grow next to woodland, so seagrass beds are often linked to other coastal marine habitats. In many places they occur alongside mangroves, growing where the water is too deep for those trees to survive. They also fringe salt marshes and coral reefs in some places, and many creatures move between them as they grow or their particular needs change.

The dense cover provided by seagrass suits many young fish. Beds off Alaska are home to shoals of tiny salmon and cod, for example, while those off Britain provide nurseries for flounder, plaice, dab and other flatfish. Many seahorses and pipefish spend their lives among seagrass, feeding on tiny creatures that live in the water. With their long, slender bodies, pipefish are almost perfectly camouflaged here. Seahorses, to which they are closely related, use their unique prehensile tails to hold on to the blades for support.

Page 82: *In a few places in the world's oceans, seagrass and kelp grow together.*

Page 83: *Unlike kelp, which are a type of algae, seagrasses are true plants with more complex tissues and developed root systems.*

Above: *A moray eel lurks in wait for prey among blades of seagrass near the shores of the Red Sea.*

Right: *There are more than 50 different species of seagrass around the world. This is neptune grass, growing off the island of Malta in the Mediterranean Sea.*

Other creatures than fish use seagrass beds as nurseries. Some bivalve molluscs settle in them as larvae, finding safety among the swaying blades. Off the eastern seaboard of the USA, the larvae of mussels and bay scallops, although mobile, settle temporarily in seagrass beds. They feed on nutrients from the leaves themselves, only letting go when when they are ready to mature and develop into filter feeding adults.

Seagrass also provides food for larger creatures. Coastal ducks such as wigeon and brent geese graze on exposed beds at low tide and other animals rely on it as their main food underwater. Adult green turtles, for instance, eat little else. These hefty creatures are the only purely herbivorous sea turtles and they rely heavily on seagrass beds to survive. Unlike other sea turtles, which hunt, they have beaks with finely serrated edges to help them more easily tear off blades of their food as they graze.

The largest of all seagrass specialists is the dugong. A close relative of the manatees, this 12-foot (3.6m) long sea cow is found only in areas where seagrass grows. While manatees inhabit rivers and estuaries as well coastal waters, the dugong is entirely marine, making it the sole herbivorous mammal to be found only at sea.

Dugongs eat the blades of seagrass but prefer the more nutritious rhizomes, which spread just beneath the surface. When feeding, they dig up the seabed with their flattened muzzles, earning them the alternative name of 'sea pigs'. Although they have only small, peg-like teeth, they chew their food before swallowing, using rough horny pads on the upper and lower palates of their jaws.

Dugongs are found on the seagrass beds of the Indian and south-western Pacific Oceans, ranging along the East African coast from Mozambique to the Red Sea, off north-western India and Sri Lanka, and around the Indo-Pacific from Indonesia, Taiwan and the Philippines to New Guinea, Australia and New Caledonia. Shy creatures that often inhabit turbid waters, they are rarely seen, but they are known to travel and feed both singly and in groups sometimes containing several hundred individuals.

Compared with other coastal habitats, seagrass beds are little studied and poorly understood. They are, however, very important, not only to marine life but also to the livelihoods of many people and the security of coastal town economies. The entire Pacific herring fishing industry relies indirectly on them, for example. Seagrass beds provide spawning grounds for these commercially important fish, which lay their eggs on the blades.

While seagrass has a vital role to play, it is threatened in many places, partly because it goes unrecognized and partly because it is so easily destroyed. Coastal construction, dredging, herbicide and fertilizer run-off, pleasure boating and dragnet fishing can all cause it to die back and even disappear completely. What is more, some seagrass species are prone to a wasting disease, the spread of which around the world has been exacerbated by shipping.

Above: Seahorses are common in seagrass beds. These little fish are unusual in that the male holds the fertilized eggs in a special pouch on the front of his body and releases the youngsters when they hatch.

Right: Seagrass grows most thickly in shallow water. Like all plants, it needs light from the sun to survive.

Previous pages: The dugong is a seagrass specialist, churning up the sea bottom to get at the plants' rhizomes, which it prefers.

Above: Sea lions rest among seagrass off the southern coast of Australia.

Left: The double-ended pipefish mimics seagrass to camouflage itself and sways with the blades in the current. Pipefish are close relatives of seahorses and, like them, feed on tiny animals which they suck into their tube-shaped mouths.

Right: Some seagrasses have strappy leaves. Others, like this Scouler's surf-grass growing off the coast of California, are more wiry.

Previous pages: A bottlenose dolphin swims over seagrass near Roatan Island in the

Left: *Green turtles, the most vegetarian of their kind, are among the most common large animals on seagrass beds in the tropics. Like all turtles, they must rise to the surface occasionally to take a breath of air. Green turtles have long, muscular tails, as this picture shows.*

Above: *A conch, its shell covered in algae, moves slowly through a bed of turtle grass. Conches are among the largest of all gastropod molluscs, the group that includes land-living slugs and snails. Like their terrestrial cousins, conchs are plant-eaters.*

Coral reefs

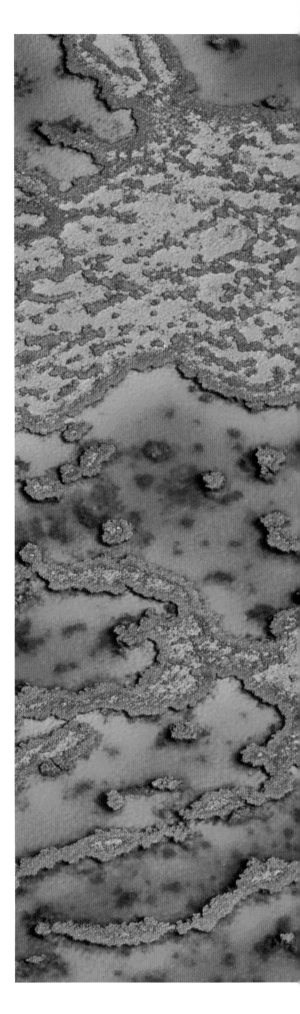

Coral reefs fringe many of the world's tropical shores like beautiful submarine gardens. Rightly famed for their colour and abundance of life, they are perhaps the most familiar of all undersea habitats, known to people around the globe, even those who have never so much as visited the ocean.

Although many of them resemble plants, the corals that make up reefs are built by animals known as polyps. Each one of these looks like a tiny sea anemone, complete with stinging tentacles. The polyps secrete the hard mineral calcium carbonate around their bodies to protect them from fish and other predators. Coral polyps that live in colonies, as most of them do, end up building fantastic structures that grow year by year. As individual polyps die they are succeeded by new ones, which extend the stony structures still further.

The shapes built by corals are many and varied, and each unique to individual species. Some resemble antlers, some fans and others brains. All, however, have one thing in common – a large surface area facing the sun. The reason for this is that the coral polyps themselves contain algae and algae need sunlight in order to produce food. By day, the polyps are sustained entirely by the sugars their algae produce. At night, when most fish and other coral predators are at rest, they extend their tentacles into the water to catch plankton and any other small particles of food that might drift by.

The close interdependence between polyps and their algae serves both partners very well indeed. Despite the huge wealth of life they support, coral reefs are actually most common in clear waters that are very low in nutrients. Without the algae, polyps alone would be hard

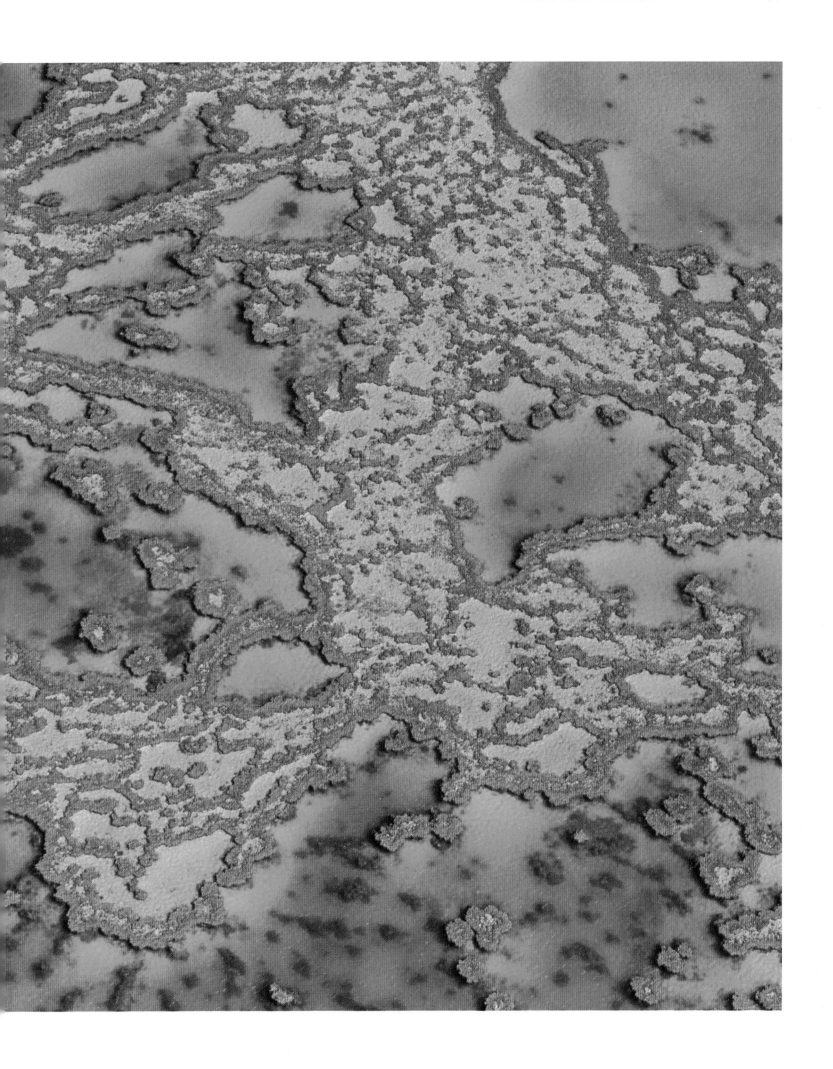

pressed to find enough food to survive. For their part the algae obtain protection from zooplankton which might otherwise eat them, nutrients in the form of some of the waste products of the polyps' metabolism, and a safe platform with excellent access to sunlight. In fact, the interdependence is so complete that coral species that contain algae cannot live without them. When rising water temperatures cause the phenomenon known as 'bleaching,' where polyps inadvertently shed their algae, these corals die. By the same token, they only occur where enough sunlight penetrates for their algae to photosynthesize. At depths below around 100 feet (30m) they start to disappear.

Unusually high water temperatures, above 82°F (28°C), cause corals to lose their internal algae and die, but equally, low temperatures inhibit most species from growing. Where surface water temperatures fall below 64°F (18°C) they are unable to survive. For this reason, most coral reefs are restricted to a band that extends around 20° north and south of the equator. The exceptions are those formed by cold-water corals in the deep sea. These live without algae, as the waters they inhabit contain enough nutrients for them to survive by catching plankton alone.

Page 96: *A yellow tang swims over coral in the Pacific Ocean.*

Page 97: *Seen from the air, the Great Barrier Reef shows its true nature. Although considered a single structure, it is made up of millions of individual corals gathered into coral heads.*

Right: *Coral reefs are sometimes called the rain forests of the sea and the comparison is apt. Like rain forests, these marine habitats are home to huge numbers of animal species.*

Below: *The Blue Hole, a famous dive site in the Belize Barrier Reef. Lying in the Caribbean Sea, the Belize Barrier Reef is the world's second largest animal-built structure, after the Great Barrier Reef.*

Coral reefs are assemblages of coral colonies and can reach a tremendous size. The largest of all reefs is the Great Barrier Reef, which stretches along the north-eastern coast of Australia. It measures more than 1200 miles (1931km) from one end to the other, making it the largest single animal-built structure on Earth and the only one that can be seen with the naked eye from space. Far less famous but also mightily impressive is the Belize Barrier Reef, which lies in the Caribbean Sea off Central America. It stretches for almost 200 miles (322km).

Corals do not just create barrier reefs, they also build fringing reefs and atolls. Fringing reefs form along coastlines and around islands, beginning just beyond the low-tide line, sometimes feet from the beach. Atolls begin life as fringing reefs that form around volcanic islands. If the islands subside or the sea rises they continue to grow until they are the only evidence left that the islands themselves ever existed. Most coral atolls are ring shaped and each tend to surround a shallow lagoon, itself filled with living coral. Parts of these ring-shaped reefs gather sediment and eventually become small islands themselves. Over time, palm trees and other plants become established on them.

Coral reefs are miraculous, almost self-sustaining habitats that require little from their surroundings in order to grow. Within their structures there are a huge variety of different niches and these support an unparalleled abundance of other marine life-forms. Plants are absent and, with few nutrients in the water, seaweeds are rare. Animals, however, exist in an incredible array of different forms.

Like almost every habitat in the oceans, coral reefs have their filter feeders. Sponges, bryozoans and sea squirts coat their surfaces, along with sea lilies and their mobile relatives the feather stars. Barnacles and bivalve molluscs can both be found here too. The coral reefs of the Indian and Pacific Oceans are home to the largest bivalve mollusc of all, the giant clam. This monstrous shellfish can grow to more than 3 feet (1m) across. Like the corals themselves, it supplements its diet of filtered foodstuffs with sugars produced by algae in the tissues of its flesh.

Different algae form thin mats upon the surfaces of reefs. These are eaten by gastropod molluscs such as sea hares, marine relatives of the slugs and snails that live on land. Other, more flamboyant gastropods of coral reefs include the carnivorous nudibranchs, more commonly known as sea slugs. These are often very colourful, despite the fact that they are slow moving and have no obvious means of defence. The reason that they can afford to be so garish is that many carry hidden weapons in the form of stinging cells appropriated from their sea anemone and coral prey. These pass undigested from a sea slug's gut into the surface of its skin and fire into any animal careless or ignorant enough to attack it. Those sea slugs that feed on different prey and have no stinging cells are also left alone, presumably because most predators have difficulty differentiating between them and their dangerous relatives.

There are fish that feed on coral too. Some, such as the emperor angelfish, are delicate eaters, picking off individual polyps with their small, pincer-like mouths. Others are more into wholesale destruction. Parrotfish, for example, chomp off chunks of coral with the tough beaks that give them their name. They then grind the chunks up using sets of teeth in their throats. The edible parts are digested and the rest ejected as tiny particles. Parrotfish are largely responsible for the fine, white sand that graces many of the world's tropical beaches.

The fish on coral reefs are spectacular, as anybody who has snorkelled over or dived on one will attest. They seem to come in every colour of the rainbow, from the powder blue and dazzling yellow of surgeonfish to the vivid reds and oranges of squirrelfish and their relatives. Many coral reef fish have scales of several colours forming distinctive patterns. The reason for this variety is uncertain, although many believe that it has to do with the sheer number of different species to be found in any one place on a reef at a time. By having a uniform unlike anyone else's, fish are more easily able to identify others of their own kind, a vital factor if they are to locate mates with which to breed.

Previous pages: *A cup coral consumes a juvenile octopus in the Red Sea. Corals belong to the same group of animals as sea anemones and jellyfish. Like them, they have tentacles that contain stinging cells, which they use to capture prey. Unlike most corals, which form colonies, cup corals are solitary and attach themselves to the surface of the reef.*

Below: *Clown anemone fish live among the tentacles of sea anemones on coral reefs in the Pacific and Indian Oceans. There are 27 different species of these fish, each with its own distinguishing pattern of coloured bands.*

The relationship coral polyps have with their algae is a type of symbiosis. Two organisms that are unrelated have come together for the mutual benefit of both. Symbiotic relationships are common on coral reefs, although few are quite as close as those of coral polyps and their algae, which rely on one another to survive.

One example of symbiosis seen on many reefs involves certain shrimps and fish. These provide a service to other, usually larger animals, by removing their parasites. The cleaner fish and cleaner shrimps benefit by getting easy meals. Their 'clients' also come out of the experience better off. Indeed, in many places they virtually queue up to have the parts they themselves cannot reach seen to.

Although symbiotic relationships are usually good for both partners, there are occasions where only one animal gains any obvious benefit. Clown anemone fish, for instance, gain protection from the tentacles of the sea anemones they inhabit but their hosts appear to get nothing in return. The fish are immune to the anemones' normally deadly weapons because their skin produces a mucus containing chemicals that stop the stinging cells from firing.

Above: The clown triggerfish inhabits reefs in the Indian and Pacific Oceans.

Below: A Nassau grouper patrols a coral reef in the Caribbean Sea. Groupers are among the largest predatory fish on coral reefs.

Seeking protection in the arms of an anemone is one way to avoid predators. Other reef fish travel in shoals to reduce their chances of being caught. Coral reefs have no shortage of predators but during the day most creatures are relatively safe. It is after nightfall that the reef's most fearsome inhabitants come out.

Moray eels may definitely be counted among this group. By day these massive, sinuous predators lie holed up in small caverns and crevices, but when darkness comes they emerge to scour the reef for prey. Their mouths contain vicious, backward-pointing teeth to hold on to the fish and other creatures on which they feed. They miss little, even on moonless nights, thanks to their extraordinarily fine-tuned sense of smell.

Moray eels hunt by stealth but blacktip reef shark attacks are more frenzied. These streamlined hunters spend the day cruising just off the edge of the reef and move in at night to find prey. Although quite large, sometimes exceeding 7 feet (2m) long, they are extremely agile and can ram their snouts into surprisingly small gaps. They hunt by frightening smaller fish into the open, often attacking in disorganized packs. Once clear of the coral there is no escape, as the sharks compete fiercely for their mouthful of food.

Other night prowlers include the several species of octopus that inhabit coral reefs. These, like morays, tend to spend the daylight hours in crevices, their flexible bodies enabling them to squeeze through all but the tightest gaps. Octopuses are molluscs, members of the same group of animals as scallops and snails, yet experiments have shown them to be unusually intelligent. Some species can also change their colour to match their background, a useful trick for avoiding predators if caught in the open and for creeping up on prey.

With their stony structures, coral reefs have an air of permanence about them. Many are indeed extremely old: carbon dating has shown that some have existed for thousands of years. However, coral reefs are not indestructible. They can be damaged and even killed off completely.

Threats to coral reefs include cyanide and dynamite fishing. Cyanide is used by divers to capture live fish for the aquarium trade and for restaurants in China. The cyanide stuns the fish but gradually works its way out of its body. However, it kills the coral in the small area in which the fish is caught. Dynamite fishing is even more destructive. Fishermen throw sticks of dynamite overboard which then explode, killing and stunning fish. These float to the surface where they are easily collected. The reef below, however, is often completely destroyed. Although both cyanide and dynamite fishing are illegal in most countries they are still techniques widely used, particularly on Indo-Pacific coral reefs.

Bleaching is another problem facing coral reefs and one that may become increasingly serious as sea temperatures rise as a result of global warming. Once they have lost their symbiotic algae, coral polyps cannot reabsorb them and they and the reefs they live on die.

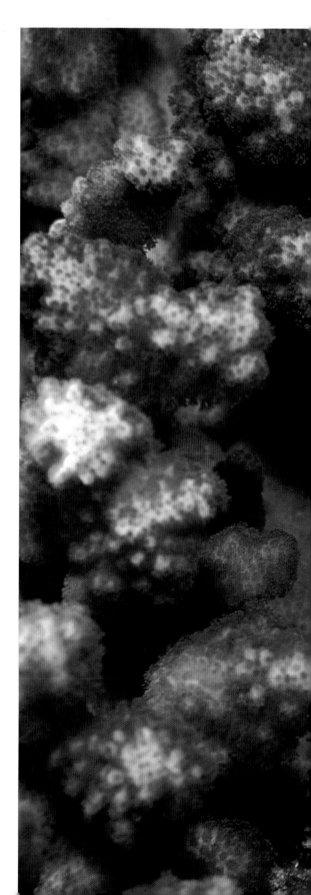

Below: *A young crown-of-thorns starfish creeps towards a cauliflower coral, which may provide its next meal. Crown-of-thorns starfish can grow to become as large as 16 inches (40cm) across. The spines which give them their name contain poison, protecting them from most marine predators.*

The other major threat to coral reefs comes from a natural predator, the crown-of-thorns starfish. In recent decades there have been several population explosions of this coral-eating starfish, devastating huge areas of reef. Although these may be part of a natural cycle, some scientists believe that they are the result of human interference. The giant triton, the crown-of-thorns' main predator, has been driven almost to the edge of extinction by shell collectors.

Above: A blacktip and a whitetip reef shark patrol the edge of a coral reef. Despite the presence of these formidable predators, most of the surrounding fish are unperturbed. Both of these species do the vast majority of their hunting at night.

Right: The pink tentacles of a sea anemone wave in the current washing over a coral reef. Although anemones feed mainly on free-swimming animals, many reef creatures rely on currents to bring their food to them.

Opposite: Sea fans are a type of colonial coral found in deeper waters on the edges of reefs. Unlike the stony corals, which make up the reef itself, most lack symbiotic algae in their tissues and rely entirely on plankton and other food particles caught from the water to sustain them.

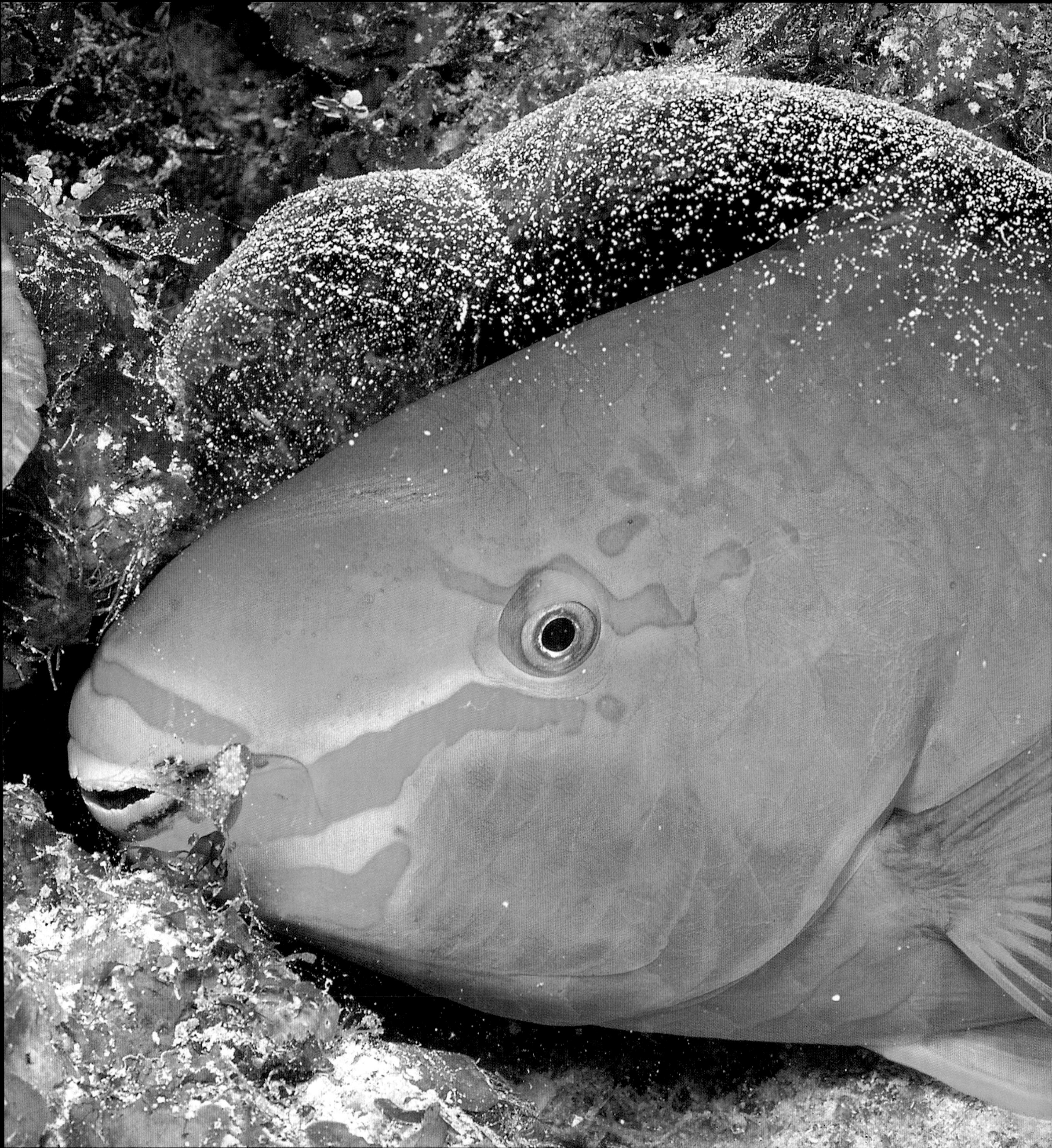

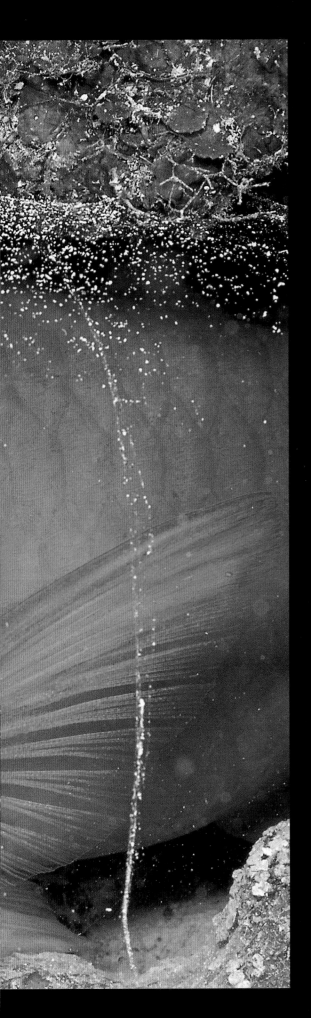

Left: *A parrotfish, resting at night in its protective cocoon, is lit by the photographer's flash. Parrotfish feed on coral, biting off chunks with their powerful beaks. When night falls, they surround themselves with a protective shield of mucus, which blocks their scent and disguises their shape from predators in the dark.*

Top: *It is not only coral reef fish that are colourful. Many crustaceans, such as this banded shrimp, wear bright costumes too.*

Above: *Many nudibranchs feed on coral polyps, incorporating the stinging cells into their own skin for defence.*

Top: Two white-eye moray eels emerge from their lair in a coral reef crevice. These formidable fish have powerful jaws, capable of taking off a diver's finger.

Above: Sponges are among the simplest of all animals. They feed by sucking water in through holes in their surface, filtering it, then pumping it out again.

Right: Two schools of fish mingle over a coral reef off Costa Rica.

Shallow seas

The world's coastal waters are among the richest habitats on earth. Here, marine life is concentrated at its greatest, the shoals of fish are thickest and the predators that hunt them most abundant. Life abounds here partly because of the relative shallowness of the waters. The tiny algae and other photosynthesizing organisms receive adequate sunlight and a constant supply of nutrients churned up from the bottom and washed off the land. Plankton thrives and blooms, providing a firm base for a rich and complex food chain.

Some creatures spend their lives in coastal waters, while others are drawn in to take advantage of seasonal gluts of food. Among the residents are several species of porpoise and dolphin. These marine mammals, smaller relatives of the great whales, are well suited to life here. Like all mammals, they breathe air, so they spend a lot of time near the surface. The fact that the waters are not especially deep is no disadvantage – in reality, it is the opposite. In many places they are able to reach the bottom and also search for food there.

Most dolphins and porpoises are sociable mammals, living in close-knit pods of related individuals which work together to find food. They locate prey using echolocation, sending out pulses of sound and then listening for the telltale echoes that bounce back off prey. Echolocation also helps them find their way around, enabling them to navigate and avoid underwater obstacles even in turbid water. It means that, although quite large, they can safely explore most nooks and crannies. They can even use it to find food hidden under sand on the seabed.

Dolphins and porpoises also use sound to communicate and keep their groups together. When hunting, many species fan out to scan a

larger area of sea. If one individual finds food, it calls the other members of its pod in. In open water fish is the usual prey, although other shoaling creatures such as squid are eaten. Once gathered, the pod works together to corral its prey and make sure that none escapes. Shoaling fish are circled and driven towards the surface, which acts as an invisible barrier to their escape. Once the shoal has tightened into what is known as a bait ball, the pod members take turns shooting in to grab a mouthful of fish. All the while, the rest of the pod keeps circling underneath and around the bait ball to hold it together. In their desperate efforts to escape some fish jump at the surface and individual pod members also break the waves to refill their lungs with air. All of this activity draws the attention of sea birds and they too arrive to join in the feast. Sharks are also often attracted by the taste of fish blood in the water. Once the feeding frenzy has finished there may be no fish left. Only those that manage to break away from the bait ball and head for deeper water escape.

Different parts of the world are home to different dolphin and porpoise species. The harbour porpoise, for instance, lives along the coasts of North America, Europe and Japan, while Burmeister's porpoise is found only around South America. Dolphins and porpoises differ little physically, although porpoises tend to be smaller and lack a prominent beak. They also live and hunt in smaller groups and are less acrobatic

Page 112: *A killer whale breaches within sight of the shore. Killer whales are social animals and work together to capture prey.*

Page 113: *A school of chevron barracuda off Sipidan Island, Malaysia. Barracuda are high-speed, predatory fish. Their fearsome reputation is largely undeserved – they very rarely attack humans unless provoked.*

Below: *Dusky dolphins play in the waters off New Zealand's South Island. Dusky dolphins are among the most acrobatic of all dolphins and are true coastal specialists. As well as New Zealand, they are found off the shores of South Africa and the southern half of South America.*

than dolphins. Peale's dolphin and the black dolphin share much of the range occupied by Burmeister's porpoise. This is not unusual. In fact, most of the world's coasts support more than one local species. In many places they are joined by others which have a more global range. The bottlenose dolphin, for example, occurs along coasts in much of the world.

The most widespread dolphin is one few people know to be a dolphin at all, the killer whale. Despite its name, this spectacular animal is not a true whale at all but the largest of all dolphin species. Like its relatives, the killer whale is a social hunter that lives and travels in family groups. It exists throughout the world's oceans, from the high Arctic and Antarctic to the equator, making it the world's most widely distributed mammal.

Killer whales are divided into two groups by biologists, residents and transients. Although members of the same species, these two groups differ markedly in their behaviour. Residents tend to form large pods, hunt vocally and occupy relatively small home ranges. These are the killer whales most often seen around shores. Transients, on the other hand, travel widely in small groups and usually hunt in silence. The reason for this is that their prey consists mainly of whales and other dolphins, creatures that would be alerted to their presence by sound.

Killer whales hunt a huge variety of prey, more than almost any other creatures in the sea. Coastal residents tend to specialize and pods have particular favourite prey species. Often they completely ignore animals they would be perfectly capable of catching. Other dolphins seem to

Top: Sea lions differ from true seals in several respects. One of the most noticeable differences is that they have visible ears. Male sea lions grow several times larger than females, the result of evolutionary pressure, as males fight one another for the right to mate and father the next generation.

sense this indifference and in many places they actually travel with killer whale pods and join their hunts.

Some resident killer whales prefer to eat salmon and other large fish and hunt them cooperatively in much the same way as other dolphins do. Other pods concentrate on larger prey, such as seals and sea lions. On the Atlantic coast of South America some even beach themselves in order to catch such prey playing in the surf.

Seals and sea lions, of course, comprise the other major groups of marine mammals found in coastal waters. The two differ slightly in their physical make-up. Sea lions, or eared seals as they are more accurately known, have muscular front and rear flippers and are able to lift their bodies up off the ground when they are out of the water. As the name of their group suggests, they also have visible external ears. True seals lack ear flaps and can only shuffle along out of water. Both groups have long whiskers to help them find prey in deep or murky waters.

Most seals and sea lions feed mainly on fish. These are caught individually, with the animals following every twist and turn to catch their prey. The majority of species breed colonially on beaches, sometimes forming colonies several thousand strong.

Many of the fish of shallow seas are most familiar to us as food. Cod and haddock both live near to the seabed in waters over the continental shelf. In some areas they may be caught within sight of the shore. Flatfish such as plaice and sole also live in coastal waters. As fry, these bottom dwellers look much like any other young fish, but as they grow older they change. The right eye migrates around to the other side of the head and the right half of the fish changes colour, eventually becoming its underside. In essence, as adults they flatten and lie on one side.

Fish and other creatures that live on the bottom are hunted by small sharks. In Atlantic waters these include dogfish, tope and smooth hounds. Other seabed predators include conger eels and rays. Some, such as the electric ray and torpedo, generate powerful electric charges within their muscles, which they fire to stun and capture small fish.

The waters above are home to shoaling fish. Mackerel, herring, pilchards and anchovies all filter the sea for plankton, concentrating where it is thickest into clouds of bodies that block out the light. Such great concentrations of fish attract predators from far and wide. Sea birds such as gannets flock to such shoals, diving into them from the air like guided missiles. Dolphins and sharks are also drawn in, along with the occasional whale. Bryde's whales, fin whales and humpbacks all feed on fish, as does the sei whale, the world's second largest animal. All four of these species are ocean wanderers that take advantage of seasonal abundances of food in coastal waters. Another, much smaller whale, the minke, however, lives on such coastal fish all the year round.

The shallow waters around shores in the subtropics are home to one of the most feared animals in the sea, the great white shark. This mon-

Above: Sardines are filter feeders that use their gills to sieve out food. They shoal in huge numbers in coastal waters, following blooms of plankton on which they feed.

strous creature is the world's largest predatory fish, reaching a staggering 20 feet (6m) long and weighing as much as 2 tons/tonnes.

Great whites feed mainly on large prey, including other sharks, dolphins, marine turtles and seals. They attack most of their prey from below, powering up from the depths with jaws wide to smash into their victims, killing or disabling them with a single, massive bite. Despite their reputation as ferocious and bloodthirsty killers, great whites are careful to avoid the risk of injury when they feed. After making their initial attack, they retreat and wait for prey to weaken from blood loss. Only when their victims have stopped struggling do they return to eat.

The great white is notable for its attacks on humans. Over the years more people have been killed by this species than by any other type of shark. The figures, however, are much lower than most people think – fewer than 100 deaths and 300 attacks in total since records began. This contrasts strikingly with the numbers notched up by a much less frequently reported coastal killer, the saltwater crocodile. It is thought to be responsible for at least 1000 human deaths every year.

Following pages: The great white shark is the world's largest predatory fish. It stalks the waters near shores in search of seals and other large prey. Schools of fish, too small to be of interest to great whites, often travel in their wake, using the sharks to protect them from other predators.

Below: Shoaling fish attract humans as well as natural predators. Here, fishermen bring in their sardine nets in Pampatar Bay off Venezuela's Margarita Island.

Above: *Like their larger cousins, killer whales, short-finned pilot whales occur both in coastal and offshore waters. Some populations are sedentary, such as those around Hawaii and the Canary Islands, but others range widely in search of the fish and squid on which they prey. Short-finned pilot whales have a largely tropical distribution. Their close relatives, long-finned pilot whales, are found in more temperate waters.*

Right: *The basking shark is the world's second largest fish, after the whale shark. Like the whale shark it is a filter feeder, swimming through clouds of plankton with its mouth open and sifting food out using its gills. Basking sharks feed in deep as well as shallow water. They are often seen off the western coast of Scotland and in the Irish Sea.*

Left: Bat rays feed on the seabed but can often be found swimming through open water, moving gracefully with flaps of their large pectoral wings. They eat shellfish and crustaceans, which they crush with their batteries of flat, plate-like teeth. Bat rays can grow to have a wingspan of almost 6.5 feet (2m), although generally speaking they are smaller than this.

Top: Electric rays lie in wait on the seabed for small fish to approach. When their prey is in range they rapidly envelop it with their disc-shaped bodies and fire off an electric charge to stun or kill it before feeding.

Above: Conger eels inhabit the seabed of the continental shelf, resting by day in crevices and emerging at night to feed.

Above: Jacks are common predators in coastal waters, particularly in the tropics. Like barracudas, they often travel in shoals, hunting down smaller fish. Many people consider jacks good eating and in some parts of the world they are fished commercially.

Right: The killer whale, also known as the orca or grampus, is a formidable predator. Coastal populations tend to feed on fish and other smaller prey but oceanic groups have been known to harry and kill much larger whales.

Chapter 3
The Open Ocean

Clear Water

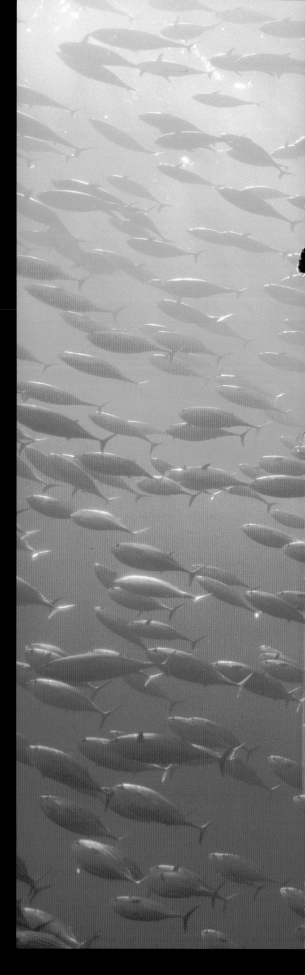

Open ocean covers well over half of the Earth. Seen from space, it dominates the planet. Most scientists consider the open ocean habitat to be those sunlit waters which lie outside the polar regions and beyond the continental shelf. As such, it is the second biggest of all the world's habitats after the deep sea.

In many ways, the open ocean is the marine equivalent of desert. Compared with coastal waters it is low in nutrients and supports relatively little life. As in terrestrial deserts, there are oases: spots where currents well up or surface water is swept from the coasts out to sea. But these oases tend to shift and the life they feed shifts with them. Only where there are strong, continuous currents, such as the Gulf Stream, does plankton occur in any reliable abundance.

The shifting nature of food in the open ocean dictates the lives of many of the animals that live there. Plankton feeders gather where it blooms and follow it as it disperses. For a short while the predators drawn in have no problem finding prey but that soon changes. In order to survive, they must often travel long distances through the sea in search of new sources of food.

In the well-lit waters of the open ocean there is nowhere to hide. Fish instead form shoals for safety and have streamlined bodies built for speed. Many are also cryptically coloured to help them blend in with the background. For predators to catch these fish they must be even faster. Most also have fine eyesight for following the movements of their prey at close quarters, as well as other senses for detecting it from distance in the vastness of the sea.

As well as the quickest swimmers, the open ocean is home to the world's largest animals. Size is a great asset where long distances have to be covered and the best advantage taken of scattered but concentrated sources of food.

Right: Skipjack tuna cruise through open water. Tuna are streamlined predators built for speed. Skipjack tuna are medium-sized members of this group, growing to around 3 feet (1m) long.

Where the wind blows

The scale of the open ocean is so great that it can be hard to grasp. Water continues on almost endlessly over the horizon, uniform, featureless and often seemingly devoid of life.

Of course appearances can be deceptive and our eyes looking down on the surface are restricted in what they can see. What may look to an observer aboard ship like a homogeneous mass of water often has areas where temperature and nutrient content vary greatly. These invisible features have a huge impact on the amount of life that may be found.

The areas of most consistently high nutrient levels in the open ocean are those where surface currents flow. These rivers in the sea are maintained by prevailing winds and carry nutrient-laden water from coastal regions sometimes for thousands of miles. Perhaps the best known of these surface currents is the Gulf Stream, which flows across the North Atlantic. It starts life in the Gulf of Mexico, hence its name, and drifts all the way to Britain and the Norwegian Sea.

The amount of water transported by the Gulf Stream is truly immense. Its volume is around 500 times that of the Amazon, the greatest river on Earth. As well as nutrients, it carries warmth, affecting the entire climate of northern Europe. The impact it has may be illustrated by the fact that subtropical plants are grown outdoors through the winter on the Isles of Scilly. This small archipelago just off the English coast lies on the same latitude as Newfoundland, which is surrounded by pack ice for much of the year.

The effect the Gulf Stream has on the open ocean is equally striking. Within its bounds, the warm, nutrient-rich water supports an abundance of animals. Beyond them, life is sparse.

What goes for the Gulf Stream is true for almost all surface currents in the open ocean. They flow literally like rivers of life through the otherwise virtually barren surface waters. The nutrients they carry feed phytoplankton, the tiny algae and other photosynthesizing organisms small enough to live suspended near the surface.

Microscopic and confined to aquatic habitats, phytoplankton is unfamiliar to most people and is often overlooked. Its contribution to life on Earth, however, is enormous. More than half of all the oxygen in the atmosphere is produced by phytoplankton. Without it, most life on land, including our own species, would be unable to survive. In the open ocean, phytoplankton forms the base of the entire food chain and, as such, is responsible either directly or indirectly for the survival of all the animals that live there.

Because of the abundance of phytoplankton, ocean surface currents are also havens for planktonic animals. Some of these, such as most copepods, spend their lives as creatures too small to see. Others later grow into larger, more familiar sea creatures. Many marine invertebrates have planktonic larvae, including bottom-living worms, filter-feeding molluscs such as mussels, and crustaceans, ranging from barnacles to prawns and crabs. The young of these creatures are not only sustained by the food they find in ocean surface currents, they are also transported by them to colonize new areas.

Page 130: Waves grow as they cross the open ocean, built up by prevailing winds.

Page 131: Waves move through surface water rather than with it. The water particles within a wave move in a rough circle as it passes, which is why floating objects bob forward and back on choppy seas rather than being pushed along.

Below: Single-celled algae and other photosynthesizing plankton form the base of the open-ocean food chain. Like the tiny planktonic animals that feed on them, they drift wherever the currents take them.

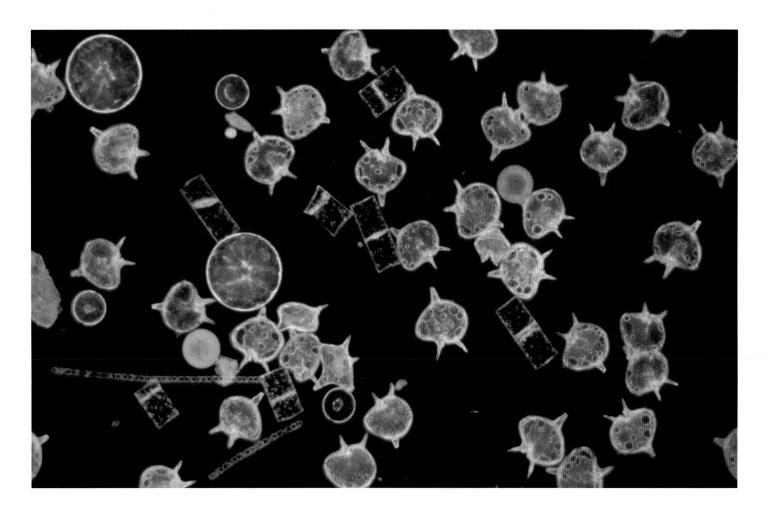

Many larger animals are also swept along by ocean currents. Swarms of jellyfish become caught up in them and are more common where they flow. Jellyfish have limited powers of movement. By rhythmically pulsing their bells they can maintain or elevate their positions in the water column, but their ability to travel horizontally through the water by their own accord is small. Most species feed on fish and other free-swimming animals, which they catch in their trailing tentacles. These tentacles contain stinging cells which immobilize and kill their prey. Once caught, food is pulled up towards the bell, which contains the mouth and digestive apparatus.

Jellyfish themselves have low nutritional value but nevertheless are the staple diet of one of the giants of the sea. The leatherback turtle, or luth, is one of the world's largest living reptiles and by far the biggest member of its group. Mature individuals can exceed nine feet (2.7m) in length and weigh almost a ton/tonne. Leatherbacks live wherever there are jellyfish to be found and follow most of the world's ocean surface currents. They also frequently dive to find food. Because of the vastness of their habitat and their relative scarcity they are rarely seen at sea, but, like all turtles, they must come ashore to lay their eggs. The largest population is in the western Atlantic and they nest on several Caribbean islands, as well as Florida and North and South Carolina on the North American mainland.

Above: Jellyfish are capable of movement but use this ability mainly to maintain their position in the water column. Like plankton, they are largely at the mercy of currents and tides.

One open ocean hunter often confused with jellyfish is the Portuguese man-o'-war. Superficially it looks very like a jellyfish with its transparent body and trailing tentacles but closer examination shows it be something very different indeed. The Portuguese man-o'-war is not actually an individual animal at all but rather a colony of different animals living and functioning as a single organism. One of these animals makes up the gas-filled float which keeps the Portuguese man-o'-war from sinking. Others form the digestive system and still others the tentacles with their stinging cells. Like the jellyfish it resembles, the Portuguese man-o'-war catches fish and other swimming creatures. Its stings are powerful enough to kill fish almost instantly and have been known to cause serious injury to humans.

Despite its fearsome underwater arsenal, the Portuguese man-o'-war is itself prey. Perhaps surprisingly, the two creatures that hunt it are molluscs. One, the violet sea snail, makes a raft of bubble-filled mucus from which it floats at the surface. The other is a floating sea slug known as *Glaucus atlanticus*. Like their prey, both of these creatures are swept along in surface currents. The sea slug is able to move slowly towards its prey, although how it detects it is uncertain. The violet sea snail, on the other hand, relies on chance to bring it and its food together.

Above: *The purple bubble raft snail spends its life at the ocean's surface, suspended beneath its self-made float. In common with jellyfish and other drifting ocean creatures, it is often washed up on beaches by the tide.*

Right: *The long tentacles of a Portuguese man-o'-war trail from the air-filled sac that keeps it afloat. A colonial organism, the Portuguese man-o'-war feeds on small fish, capturing and killing them with its tentacles, which contain deadly stinging cells.*

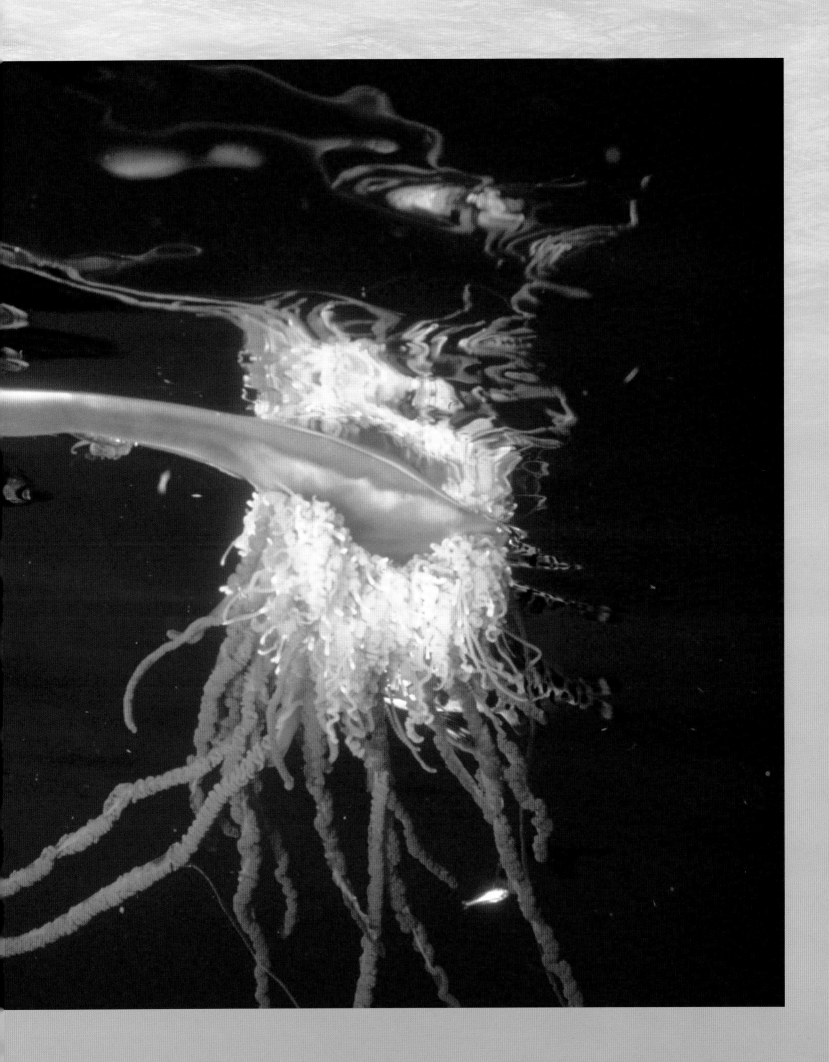

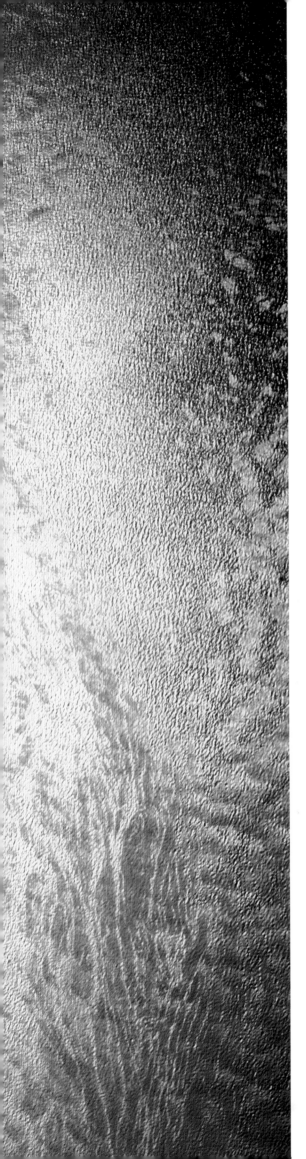

Many of the world's ocean surface currents link up to form loose circles known as gyres. They are driven by prevailing winds, which are themselves influenced by the rotation of the Earth. As a result, gyres in the Northern Hemisphere rotate in a clockwise direction. Those in the Southern Hemisphere rotate anticlockwise.

The North Atlantic Ocean has its own gyre, of which the Gulf Stream is its north-western arm. The eastern part of the gyre is made up by the Canary Current, which runs southward from western Europe to the Cape Verde Islands off Senegal in Africa. Here, the North Equatorial Current begins flowing westward across the Atlantic towards the Caribbean and the Gulf of Mexico. In the middle of the gyre, parts of the ocean are almost completely still. One such area is the Sargasso Sea, famous as the destination of western North America's and Europe's migrating freshwater eels, which travel there to breed.

The Sargasso Sea is roughly 700 miles (1126km) wide and 2000 miles (3218km) long: Bermuda lies near its western edge. Its glassy waters are filled with great rafts of sargassum seaweed, after which it is named. These provide both food and shelter for a variety of fish and other animals. The Sargasso's seaweeds are uniquely adapted to live at the surface and form a floating forest unlike any other habitat on Earth. Constrained by the huge currents that surround them, they live on the surface of the open ocean, floating more than two miles (3.2km) above the inky blackness of the seabed below.

Left: The Gulf Stream flows like a vast river across the surface of the North Atlantic Ocean. At its edge, swirls of water known as eddies sometimes form. These are so large that they can be seen from space. This picture was taken from the space shuttle Endeavour.

Above: A juvenile filefish hides among Sargassum seaweed. Unlike most seaweeds, which live attached to the shore or rocks just below the sea, Sargassum floats free at the surface. Where the water is still, such as in the Sargasso Sea, it gathers in huge quantities.

Previous pages: *Leatherback turtles follow the world's ocean currents feeding mainly on jellyfish. These huge reptiles come ashore to lay their eggs in the soft sand.*

Left: *The purple-banded jellyfish is found only in the open waters of the Pacific Ocean.*

Above: *In blustery weather the sea's surface is whipped up and whitecaps form. The whiteness is caused by bubbles at the surface and droplets above it reflecting the sunlight that falls on them.*

Following pages: *Islands provide outposts of life for humans and nesting sites for sea birds in the open ocean. This picture shows Bermuda, which lies near the northern edge of the Sargasso Sea.*

Safety in numbers

The clear, sunlit waters of the open ocean offer animals nowhere to hide. Survival here for most is all about escaping predators rather than avoiding them. The best way to do that is to crowd together. Other bodies provide a modicum of cover and individuals in a shoal are harder for predators to pick out.

Most open water fish travel in large shoals for this reason. If they are discovered they bunch together, seemingly reacting to movement as one. This apparent group behaviour is actually each individual's instinctive response to danger. Any fish caught on its own outside the shoal is almost certain to be picked off, hence the bunching. The coordinated movement may look intelligent, as if some form of communication is involved, but in fact it is not. Studies of slowed-down footage have shown that each fish simply follows and mimics the movement of the one in front of it. The reactions are so fast that, seen in normal time, the entire shoal appears to move almost as one.

Many shoaling fish are coloured or patterned to help make them more difficult for predators to pick out. Silvery sides reflect light and appear to make their bodies blur together. Some open water fish have additional camouflage to make them harder to spot from above. Mackerel, for example, have bodies that are mostly silver, but their upper sides are covered by iridescent blue and green stripes. This helps them blend in with the rippling surface of the sea, making them harder for sea birds to target or spot from the air.

Colour can help animals to avoid detection in open water but the best way to do this is to have no colour at all. Transparency is rare among fish and mainly occurs in freshwater species. Many marine invertebrates are

transparent, however. Among the largest and best known of these creatures are jellyfish. Being transparent helps them not only to avoid predators but also to catch prey. If their trailing tentacles were opaque, they
would be much easier for fish to spot and avoid.

There are over 200 species of jellyfish known to science and doubtless
many more that remain to be discovered. All are mobile as adults but go
through a smaller, stationary polyp stage before reaching maturity. The
vast majority of species are carnivorous but some, like their relatives the
tropical hard corals, contain symbiotic algae in their body tissues. A few
species obtain all of their food from this source.

Most jellyfish live within the water column, staying near the surface
by pulsing their bell-shaped bodies. One species, however, has developed
a different way to prevent itself sinking. Known as the by-the-wind-sailor,
it has an air-filled float. By-the-wind sailors feed on small animals that
live at the ocean's surface, using their short tentacles to catch their prey.
They move by catching the wind with a 'sail' of transparent tissue on the
tops of their bodies. Like other jellyfish, they often form large swarms.

Page 144: Virtually all but the largest open-ocean fish form schools. In a place with no cover, the bodies of others provide some protection from attack.

Page 145: Yellow-banded snappers, or hussars, are confined to the western Pacific Ocean off Australia and New Caledonia.

Below: Currents often force jellyfish together in large numbers. These swarms attract predators such as leatherback turtles, which follow ocean currents to locate their prey.

Comb jellies resemble jellyfish but are not closely related to them. They too have transparent bodies and live in surface waters, where they feed on plankton. Comb jellies are smaller than most jellyfish and, unlike them, do not have stinging cells. Where plankton blooms they may form large swarms, although these are invisible from anything more than a few feet away.

Salps, like comb jellies, feed on plankton. They are not true invertebrates but instead belong to a group of animals known as the tunicates, which lie between the invertebrates and the vertebrates in evolutionary terms. Unlike true vertebrates, they do not have a backbone but they do have the rudiments of a spinal cord. They move through the water by contracting their transparent, muscular, barrel-shaped bodies.

Salps have a complicated life cycle with alternating generations of sexually and asexually reproducing forms. The former live in colonies of joined individuals, forming long strings, spirals or wheel shapes in the ocean's surface waters. The offspring they create live and feed individually. These later reproduce by budding off miniature but complete colonies.

When conditions are right, salps can grow and reproduce extremely quickly to form swarms. Some can increase their body length by as much as 10 per cent an hour and may complete their entire life cycle in as little as two days.

Being practically invisible is one way to avoid being caught and shoaling is another. A few open-ocean fish employ a third method to escape predators – leaving the water.

Needlefish live in shoals at the water's surface. Their long, muscular bodies are extremely well streamlined and they can swim at high speeds. Even so, they are not as quick as some of the fastest open-ocean hunters.

Above: Comb jellies look superficially like jellyfish but the two groups are only very distantly related. Comb jellies, or sea gooseberries as they are also known, move by means of tiny hair-like structures called cilia, which line the ridges of their bodies. They are predators, engulfing the larvae of crustaceans and other planktonic animals. Most comb jellies are translucent but a few have pigmented bodies. None grow much larger than this species, which reaches 4 inches (10cm) long.

When they find themselves under attack from a predator they cannot outrun, needlefish leap from the water, often travelling through the air for some distance. As far as the predator chasing them is concerned, they effectively disappear as soon as they break the surface.

Another group of open-ocean fish has taken this method of escape one step further. Rather than just jumping out of the water, they spread their fins and fly, or more accurately glide, to safety. These flying fish, as they are known, inhabit warm seas worldwide, feeding on crustaceans and large planktonic animals. They are panicked into flight by movement in the water and are just as likely to be sent skimming over the waves by boats or ships as they are by predators.

Flying fish glide by means of their hugely enlarged pectoral fins. When they are swimming, these are held flat against the side of the body but they are flicked open as soon as the fish leave the water. Some also have enlarged pelvic fins, giving them four 'wings' instead of two.

Flying fish have deeply forked tails, with the lower lobe much longer than the upper. The fish use their tails in flight like outboard motors, sweeping them vigorously from side to side as soon as they dip into the water. By doing this, they can greatly extend the distance that they travel. The longest flights observed have covered well over 500 feet (150m).

More than 50 species of flying fish have been discovered so far. The largest grow up to 17 inches (43cm) long, but most are smaller, measuring less than a foot (30cm) in length.

Above: *Flying fish have huge pectoral fins which they extend like wings as they leap from the water. These carry them over the surface and out of sight of predators beneath the waves.*

Right: *Coral reefs form around seamounts whose peaks are near the surface of the open ocean. These act like underwater islands, drawing in fish, such as these blue-lined snappers, from miles around.*

Opposite: Even relatively large fish, such as these jacks, stick together in the open ocean. Only the top predators, such as sharks, can risk travelling alone.

Above: Needlefish are aptly-named denizens of clear open water. Their slender bodies are tipped with long, pointed jaws filled with sharp teeth, which they use to snap up prey near the surface. Needlefish are closely related to flying fish and, like them, sometimes leap from the water to escape larger predators. They have been known to impale themselves on the sides of wooden boats and even the occasional unfortunate fisherman.

Right: Schooling fish naturally bunch together when they sense danger. This makes it harder for predators to pick out individuals.

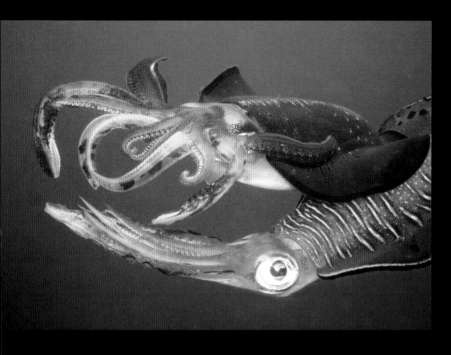

Top: Cuttlefish, and their close relatives squid, move slowly through the water by undulating the fins along their sides. They can also move more quickly by jet propulsion, squirting out water from a tube beneath the head.

Above: A killer whale circles a school of fish. Killer whales are the most widely distributed mammals in the world, occurring throughout all of the oceans, from the tropics to the poles.

Right: Most open-water fish have silver-sided bodies, which reflect surrounding light and help make them harder to distinguish in schools.

Wandering giants

The open ocean is home to the largest animals on Earth. The biggest of all is the blue whale. This titanic mammal is a creature of superlatives: almost everything about it is unmatched in the natural world. It has the largest heart of any animal, the size of a small family car. A grown man could swim down its biggest blood vessels and its tongue alone weighs more than an adult African elephant. The largest blue whale ever measured was 110 feet (33.5m) long and had an estimated weight of almost 200 tons (203 tonnes). Fossils show that some dinosaurs were slightly longer but none came close to it in mass. To the best of our knowledge, the blue whale is not only the biggest animal alive today but the biggest that has ever lived.

Despite its size, the blue whale is rarely seen. The reason for this is twofold. First of all, its habitat is so vast that it is easily hidden. Secondly, the blue whale itself is rare. Decades of hunting by whalers decimated its population and it has barely begun to recover. Like many large animals, it is a slow breeder with females giving birth no more than once every two or three years.

The blue whale is the largest of the baleen whales. All of these whales are filter feeders, sieving prey from the water with the plates of baleen that give them their name. Most baleen whales eat shoaling fish and krill – shrimp-like crustaceans that swarm in some of the world's surface waters. Their feeding method is simple: they swim through shoals and swarms with their mouths open, scooping up huge numbers of prey at a time. After taking a gulp, they close their mouths so that the curtains of baleen hanging down from their top jaws trap the prey inside. The edge of each baleen plate is fringed with long bristles which let water out but

keep fish, krill and other creatures in. By pushing upwards with the tongue, the food is strained from the water before swallowing.

Finding enough food to sustain a creature of its size takes some effort but the blue whale is a great traveller. The species has an almost global distribution, although whales tend to be more common in some areas than others, often reflecting the abundance of food. Between meals the blue whale is kept alive by the energy stored in its great mass of blubber. During the breeding season, spent in warmer, nutrient poor waters, individuals may not feed for weeks.

One might expect an animal of its size to be ponderous but the blue whale is capable of surprising turns of speed. Although it normally moves quite slowly to conserve energy it can swim at up to 20mph (32km/h). The blue whale sometimes dives to find food, although it tends to stay within the top 650 feet (198m) or so of water where sunlight penetrates. Like all mammals it breathes air and so frequently returns to the surface. Its first exhalation is known as a blow and can be seen from some distance away. Having been held within its lungs for as much as half an hour, the air is warm and moist and emerges filled with water droplets. This plume of spray can rise 30 feet (9m) above the waves.

Page 154: *The tail fins, or flukes, of a humpback whale rise from the water as it dives.*

Page 155: *Like all baleen whales, the blue whale has paired blowholes, which are held tightly shut when underwater. Dolphins and toothed whales, such as the sperm whale, have single blowholes.*

Below: *The blue whale is the largest animal ever known to have existed. The biggest can weigh up to 200 tons/203 tonnes, twice as much as the heaviest dinosaur. Blue whales, like all of the large whales, are much rarer today than they once were. Centuries of commercial hunting decimated their populations and their recovery since this was ended by most countries has been slow.*

The blue whale is one of 11 baleen whale species and one of six members of a family known as the rorquals. The name rorqual refers to the folds of skin or throat grooves that these whales have and comes from Norwegian word *rorhval*, which literally means 'furrow'. These pleats enable the throat to expand like the beak of a pelican when the whales take a gulp of food.

Although the blue whale is the world's largest animal, the fin whale runs it a close second, growing to more than 85 feet (26m) long. Like the blue whale, this rorqual has an almost global distribution, but unlike its generally solitary cousin, it lives and travels in groups. Fin whales are commonly seen in pods of three to seven but more than 100 may gather at good feeding grounds. The fin whale is also more acrobatic than the blue, with fully grown adults sometimes leaping almost right out of the water, a behaviour known as breaching.

The other four rorquals, in descending order of length are the sei whale (up to 70 feet/21m long), the humpback whale (up to 60 feet/18m long), Bryde's whale (up to 50 feet/15m long) and the minke (up to 33 feet/10m long). With one exception, all have a relatively similar appearance – discounting their size and colouration – with long, streamlined bodies perfect for cutting through the water at speed. The exception is the humpback whale, perhaps the most familiar of the rorquals and by far the best studied species.

The humpback whale is more stocky than other rorquals and has the longest flippers of any animal: exceeding 15 feet (4.5m) in length they are twice as long as those of any other whale. The humpback whale uses its

Above: *A fin whale surfaces, showing the neat, backward-curving dorsal fin that gives it its name. Despite the fact that it is the world's second largest animal and has an almost global distribution, few people have ever heard of it and even fewer have seen one: testament, perhaps, to the true vastness of the open ocean where it lives.*

Following pages: *A humpback whale rests near the surface. The humpback is one of the most commonly seen and easily recognized of the baleen whales – its enormous flippers are unlike those of any other species.*

flippers to communicate, slapping them against the water's surface, which creates a tremendous noise beneath. It also sometimes lies on its back and holds its flippers up in the air, a behaviour that appears to serve no obvious function and has long mystified biologists.

Humpback whales are perhaps most famous for their songs. Adult males make long and complex vocalizations which may last for over half an hour at a time. Composed of snores, groans, chirps, whistles and other sounds, these have identifiable patterns making them true songs, like the songs of birds. Songs are repeated, sometimes for hours, paused only for short breaks when the males return to the surface to breathe. The sounds travel for great distances and have been detected more than 100 miles (160km) away. This is partly because of their volume and partly because of the medium they are made in – sound travels much better through water than through air.

Like bird song, it is thought that humpback songs enable females to judge the quality of potential mates and also pass information to other males. Exactly how other whales make judgements based on the songs is unclear. What is known is that humpbacks have regional dialects. The songs of males in one area are very similar to one another but clearly distinct from those made by males in other parts of the sea. Songs also change subtly from year to year.

Humpbacks have the most complex songs but other whales also sing. The rather more monotonous three note song of the male blue whale is the loudest noise made by any animal on Earth. At 188 decibels, it would drown out the engine of a jet plane and travels for hundreds of miles through the water.

There are five baleen whale species other than the rorquals: the northern right whale, the southern right whale, the bowhead whale, the grey whale and the pygmy right whale. The right whales were given their name by early whalers. Because they float after death they were considered the 'right' whales to kill. The northern and southern right whales are both very similar in appearance but are geographically quite distinct. As their names suggest, the northern right whale is found only in the Northern Hemisphere and the southern right whale only in the Southern Hemisphere. Neither species ever enters tropical waters so they are always separated by several thousand miles of ocean. Northern and southern right whales have enormous mouths with lower jaws that extend upwards far above the eyes. Only the bowhead's mouth is bigger. Fully open, it is large enough to swallow a minibus. These three species of giant filter feeders form a family. The bowhead is unique in being the only exclusively Arctic baleen whale.

The pygmy right whale, despite its name, is unrelated to the other right whales and is given a family of its own by biologists. It is actually the smallest of all baleen whales, rarely reaching more than 22 feet (6.7m) long. The pygmy right whale inhabits temperate waters of the

Southern Hemisphere but is poorly studied and little known. Its size and range mean that it is less commonly seen than most baleen whales and as a result it is not even known roughly how many there are.

The grey whale, on the other hand, is closely monitored. Once hunted close to extinction, the vast majority of its global population now breeds off Baja California in north-western Mexico. The grey whale makes the longest annual migration of any mammal, travelling all the way down the western seaboard of North America during autumn then returning to the Arctic Ocean via the Bering Strait to fatten up the following summer. Grey whales live only in the North Pacific Ocean and the Chukchi Sea of the Arctic Ocean, between Alaska and Siberia. A small number migrate down the eastern coast of Russia and travel through the Sea of Japan to breed in the waters off South Korea.

Baleen whales are not the only giants of the open ocean. Other, more mysterious, large creatures live here too.

The oarfish is thought by some to be the original sea serpent of myth. With its long, sinuous body it could easily be mistaken for a giant snake. It certainly does not look like any other fish in the ocean.

Oarfish are found in all of the world's temperate and tropical seas, but they are rarely seen alive as they only occasionally come close enough to the surface to be spotted. They feed mainly by filtering planktonic animals from the water, although they also take small fish, jellyfish and squid when the opportunity arises. The longest oarfish ever reliably measured was 26 feet (8m) from nose to tail, although specimens twice that length have been reported.

Even longer than the oarfish and far more massive, the whale shark is the biggest fish in the sea. Another filter feeder, it inhabits tropical and warm temperate ocean waters, swimming through them with its mouth open like a giant funnel. The water that enters a whale shark's mouth passes out again through its open gill slits, but any animals it contained are sifted out by the shark's gill rakers. These cover the entrances to the gills slits at the back of the mouth like a fine mesh.

The whale shark grows up to 59 feet (18m) long and can weigh over 20 tons/tonnes. Its huge mouth is positioned right at the front of its head, unlike those of most sharks, which have a prominent snout with the mouth on the underside. Like many other open ocean creatures it is poorly understood, although it is thought to give birth to live young. A slow swimmer, it is generally docile and harmless to humans, even tolerating divers hitching a ride by grabbing its huge dorsal fin.

The manta ray is another filter-feeding giant of tropical waters. Like the whale shark, it has an enormous mouth and uses gill rakers to sift out its prey. The manta is by far the largest of the world's rays and one of the few species to spend its life in open water rather than on the seabed. Two enormous lobes on either side of its mouth help it direct water and prey inward as it swims along.

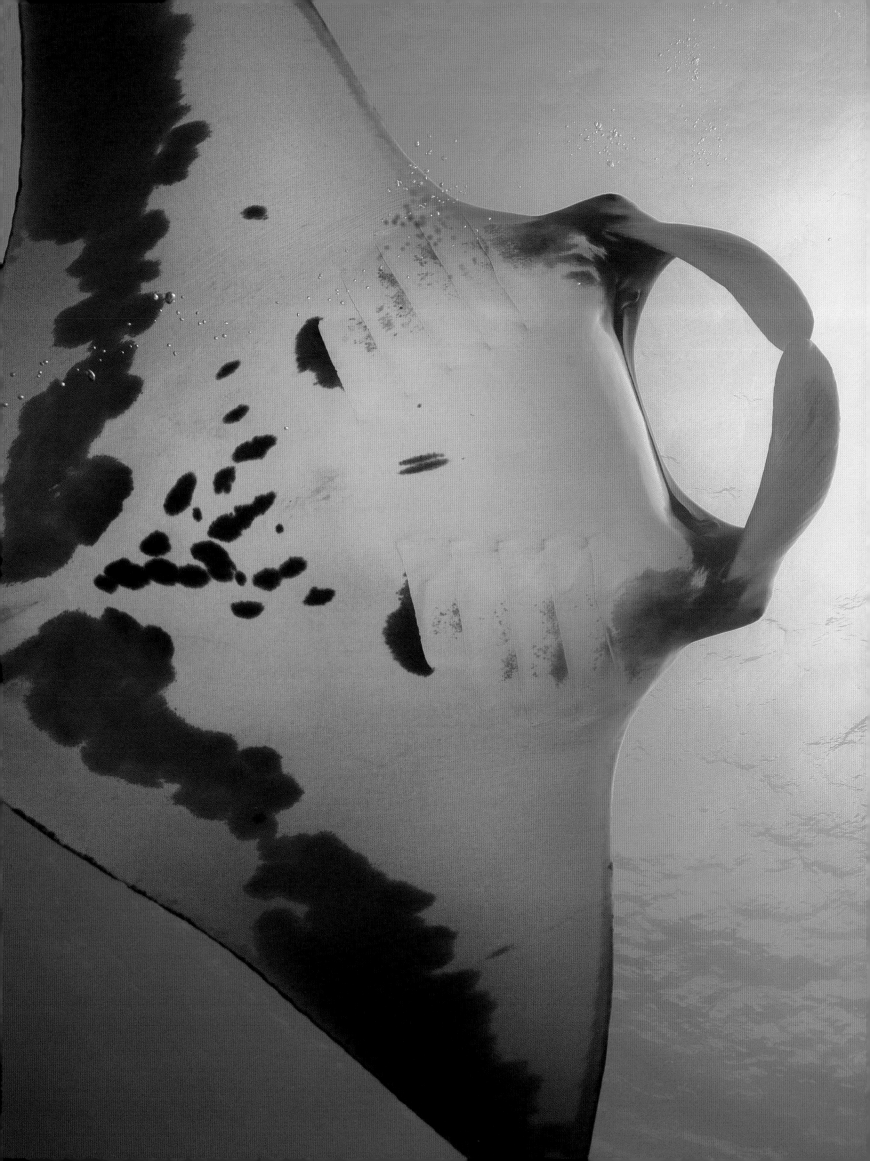

Manta rays swim by gracefully flapping the muscular 'wings' that extend out from their bodies. In large individuals, these may measure 16 feet (4.8m) from tip to tip. Where food is plentiful, manta rays often gather in large numbers. Many carry passengers in the shape of fish called remoras, which pick off bits of food the mantas miss. Remoras also gain protection from their giant hosts, as predators seem not to notice them, perhaps mistaking them for parts of the rays themselves.

It is not just manta rays that carry remoras. Many other large fish, including whale sharks, do so as well. Remoras attach themselves to their unwitting hosts by means of a powerful suction pad formed from a modified dorsal fin. Whenever they spot food, they loosen their grip and swim towards it before sticking themselves back on to their hosts again.

Sharks and rays are primitive fish with skeletons made of cartilage. Most other fish have skeletons of bone. The largest of these bony fish also lives in the open ocean and is one of the strangest looking beasts in the sea. Known as the sunfish, for its habit of basking at the surface, it has an enormous rounded, flattened body with almost no tail. It propels itself by flapping its elongated dorsal and anal fins and feeds mainly on jellyfish.

Sunfish can reach 12 feet (3.6m) long and weigh over a ton/tonne. Their closest relatives are triggerfish, boxfish and porcupine fish, all much smaller and mostly found living on coral reefs.

Above: The Oarfish has a ribbon-like body that may measure 26 feet (8m) or more in length.

Previous pages: Manta rays are the world's largest rays and the only ones to live on a diet of plankton, which they sift from the water.

Right: The whale shark is another filter feeder, which removes its food from the water using its gill slits in the same way as the manta ray. Whale sharks have also been known to feed on small fish, ploughing into schools to snap up hundreds at a time.

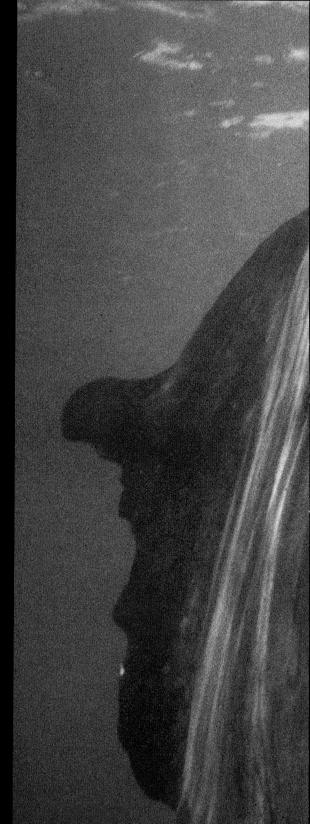

The quick and the dead

Speed is the key to survival for most predators in the open ocean. Their prey is fast so they need to be faster. The sunlit waters off-shore are home to the quickest fish in the sea, as well as the most streamlined species of dolphin.

The natural world's sprint swimming champion is the cosmopolitan sailfish. This large and beautiful fish can reach speeds of up to 68mph (109km/h). With its long, pointed snout it is shaped like a dart, the perfect design to cut effortlessly through the water. Power is provided by its long, lean, muscular body and delivered with broad sweeps of its tail. The tail fins themselves form a large V, not unlike a fighter plane's wings. As well as speed, they give the fish incredible acceleration as it charges in to capture prey.

The cosmopolitan sailfish is an impressive animal, growing up to 10 feet (3m) long. It hunts in clear waters near the surface and feeds mainly on squid and smaller fish. Its favoured prey includes tuna, jacks and needlefish, themselves all very speedy species.

Once it has located a prey shoal, the cosmopolitan sailfish rushes in, its large dorsal fin folded back into a groove on the top of its body. As it enters the shoal, it sweeps its long bill through the water with the intent of stunning or maiming its prey. Its own momentum usually brings it right out the other side, but there it turns and swims back to pick off any fish or squid that it hit.

The cosmopolitan sailfish's sail – its dorsal fin – can be raised and lowered like a flag. It is often raised when circling shoals of prey to frighten them and cause them to bunch closer together. The sailfish's skin also changes colour in pulses as it attacks, for the same reason.

The cosmopolitan sailfish inhabits tropical and subtropical waters worldwide. It shares its habitat with many similar looking species, some closely related to it and others less so. Collectively, these predators are known as billfish. They include many species highly prized by sports fishermen and gourmets, including marlin and swordfish. All hunt in the upper waters of the open ocean. Most are solitary, except when breeding, due to the scattered nature of their prey.

Other large fish in the open ocean have a similar lifestyle and have evolved along similar lines. Although they lack a spear-like bill, they too have long, streamlined, muscular bodies built for speed. One such creature is the dolphinfish.

A striking animal with a brilliant metallic blue-green body, the dolphinfish lives in tropical and subtropical waters. In common with billfish, the adults are mainly solitary but juveniles travel and hunt in small shoals. Dolphinfish hunt very close to the surface and flying fish are amongst their favourite prey. They often lie in wait beneath floating objects and are very common in the Sargasso Sea.

Dolphinfish themselves are eaten by larger open-ocean hunters, including marlin and sailfish. They are also caught in large numbers by commercial fishing vessels.

Page 166: *A swordfish swims through the open waters of the Pacific Ocean.*

Page 167: *Bottlenose dolphins are found in tropical and temperate seas, both in coastal waters and far from land.*

Opposite: *Spinner dolphins are among the most streamlined of all marine mammals. They are named after their habit of twisting on their axis in the air when they breach.*

Below: *When swimming, the cosmopolitan sailfish holds its flag-like dorsal fin flat along its back. This high-speed hunter lives in tropical and subtropical waters.*

Both of these facts are things dolphinfish have in common with tuna, perhaps the most successful group of predatory open water fish. Tuna fill the world's tropical and subtropical oceans, and several species are also found in temperate waters. Most of us encounter them as meat packaged in a can but the very abundance of this food reflects the huge numbers of them that there are out in the sea.

Tuna travel in shoals and there are several different species. The largest of all is the now endangered bluefin tuna. Historical records show that this monstrous fish can grow to 15 feet (4.5m) in length and weigh over half a ton (500kg), although most adult specimens caught today are significantly smaller, rarely exceeding 8 feet (2.4m) long. It inhabits sub-tropical and temperate waters in the Northern Hemisphere, including the Mediterranean Sea. Like all tuna, it is highly streamlined and can reach impressive speeds. Some individuals have been clocked swimming at 45mph (72km/h), while tagging studies have shown these fish crossing the entire Atlantic Ocean in less than 60 days.

Slightly smaller than bluefin tuna, yellowfin tuna live in tropical and subtropical seas. They too are fast-moving predators but form much larger shoals than bluefins, making them prime targets for fishing fleets. Yellowfin tuna tend to shoal by size rather than species and are often

Above: A diver approaches a young adult yellowfin tuna. Tuna grow almost continually throughout their lives. Individuals of similar size shoal and travel together.

Right: A blue marlin leaps from the water in hot pursuit of prey. Marlin are closely related to sailfish and, like them, are highly prized by sports fishermen.

found travelling with other similar-sized predators, such as dolphins. In the past, commercial fishermen often took advantage of this fact, homing in on large schools of dolphins – easily visible from above the surface – in order to catch the tuna travelling with them. An unfortunate side effect of this practice was that large numbers of dolphins were killed, drowned after becoming entangled in the fishermen's nets. Today most canned yellowfin tuna sold is 'dolphin-friendly' – located by other methods and caught without killing dolphins as part of the process.

Smaller than the yellowfin and even more commercially important is the skipjack tuna. This species feeds on herrings, anchovies, sardines and other small shoaling fish, including juveniles of its own kind. Skipjack tuna share the yellowfin's range but as adults the two species do not compete. The skipjack's preferred prey is smaller, reflecting its own size. Most adult skipjack tuna are under 3 feet (1m) long.

Skipjacks are themselves an important source of food for larger predators, including several types of shark. Among them is the blue shark, a solitary and nomadic species of warm and temperate seas. Like all sharks, the blue shark has an excellent sense of smell and is drawn by the slightest scent of blood in the water. If fish are under attack by other animals, dolphins for example, it is often the first to arrive and join in the feast. The blue shark also hunts for itself, charging into shoals of fish or squid at speed to snap up prey.

Above: *The mako shark is true open-water species, built for speed as well as power. It sits right at the top of the food chain, hunting other predators of a similar size.*

Opposite: *Tuna are among the most common large fish in the open ocean and often school in vast numbers. Like most other open-water fish, they are capable of incredible bursts of speed when escaping predators or chasing prey.*

The blue shark has a long, torpedo-shaped body and is widely regarded as one of the fastest sharks in the sea. There is one other shark, however, that can outrun it and indeed sometimes preys on it, the short-fin mako. If the blue shark looks fearsome, the shortfin mako is terrifying. Its long, backward-pointing teeth jut from its mouth like fangs. In common with most sharks, the shortfin mako has several rows of teeth in each jaw and continues to grow new teeth throughout its life. As those at the front fall out or become wedged in prey they are replaced by new ones, which move forward from the row behind.

The mako uses its gruesome teeth to tear chunks from its prey. Unlike the blue shark, it goes for other top predators, including swordfish and yellowfin tuna. The shortfin mako resembles the great white shark, to which it is closely related, but is smaller and more streamlined. Adult makos average from 5 feet to 8 feet (1.5m to 2.4m) long but they can grow much bigger, reaching as much as 12 feet (3.6m) long and weighing over 1000 pounds (450kg).

Another open-ocean predator and occasional prey of the shortfin mako is the thresher shark. This weird-looking creature has an enormously long tail fin, with the upper lobe as long as its head and body together. Far from being some bizarre natural curiosity, this tail fin is very functional and helps the thresher shark capture its prey. Schools of fish such as mackerel are circled then stunned with a swipe of the tail. Threshers are unusual among sharks in often working together in pairs or groups to herd their prey before attacking.

Dolphins, on the other hand, almost never hunt alone and this is as true for oceanic species as any others. More than a dozen species of dolphin live in this environment, some with overlapping ranges and others peculiar to particular oceans and seas.

The most widespread is the aptly named common dolphin, which occurs in tropical and temperate waters worldwide. It forms large schools, ranging from 10 to 500 individuals, although as many as 2000 may gather together at rich feeding grounds. In the Pacific Ocean, the common dolphin is the species most commonly found swimming with yellowfin tuna. Like those fish, it is a powerful, fast swimmer that hunts smaller fish and squid as its main prey. The common dolphin is highly acrobatic, frequently leaping from the water and sometimes turning somersaults in the air, often apparently just for the fun of it.

As they travel, common dolphins often 'porpoise' – jump from the water to grab a new breath of air on the move. Striped dolphins also do this and, if anything, are even more acrobatic. This species, which has a similar distribution to the common dolphin and often associates with it, sometimes porpoises upside down and has even been seen doing backward somersaults in the air. Striped dolphins also leap from the water higher than most other dolphins, occasionally clearing the surface by 20 feet (6m) or more.

Dolphins are famously playful and in many cases they seem to perform such acrobatics just for pleasure. Sometimes, however, they leap for more practical reasons. The noise made by a dolphin's body slapping the surface can be heard from some distance away and many scientists believe they often leap for reasons of communication, possibly to alert others to the presence of fish. A few have also suggested that leaping may help oceanic dolphins rid themselves of parasites, such as barnacles. In the open ocean there is no other way for them to scratch or knock these creatures off.

Jumping on the move, porpoising, is a way of saving energy as well as catching a breath. Air offers less resistance to movement than water, so the more time a dolphin spends flying through it, the less energy it has to expend propelling itself along.

As the name suggests, spinner dolphins porpoise in a very characteristic way, turning on their longitudinal axis several times before re-entering the water. This behaviour makes spinner dolphins very easy to recognize at sea. There are two species, both of which often gather in groups of several hundred. The long-snouted spinner dolphin occurs in tropical and subtropical seas worldwide. The short-snouted spinner dolphin is found only in the Atlantic Ocean, again in tropical and subtropical waters.

Common, striped and spinner dolphins are 'typical' dolphins with a familiar look to them. Their teardrop-shaped bodies have a prominent dorsal fin and they all have rounded foreheads and obvious beaks. In short, they look very like the bottlenose dolphin, which is the species most often kept in dolphinariums.

Other oceanic dolphins look a little more strange to most people's eyes. The rough-toothed dolphin, for instance, has a sloping forehead and snout, although in other respects it is typical. Right whale dolphins, of which there are two species, not only have sloping foreheads but also lack a dorsal fin. Their sleek appearance and the fact that they leave the water with low-angled leaps mean that from distance they look almost like sea lions or fur seals. Of course, unlike these other animals, they are hairless. Dolphins, whales and porpoises (collectively known as cetaceans) are unique in that respect among mammals.

Other oceanic dolphins lack a prominent beak. Risso's dolphin, for example, has a completely rounded head. In this respect, it closely resembles the blackfish, larger members of the dolphin family that are commonly known as whales.

Blackfish comprise six species, all of which are either partly or completely oceanic. The largest of the blackfish is the killer whale. Killer whales that live in the open ocean are known as transients, as opposed to residents (see page 115), and mainly hunt other cetaceans. These fearsome predators include the great baleen whales among their prey: they have even been observed hounding and wounding blue whales. Baleen whale calves are particularly vulnerable to killer whale attacks. Members

Opposite: *A bottlenose dolphin and her calf. Dolphins give birth near the surface and help their babies up to take their first breath. Within hours, the youngsters are able to swim alongside their mothers.*

Below: *When it is not hunting, the blue shark cruises slowly through the open ocean to save energy. Its pectoral fins act like wings, giving it lift in the water as it swims. The blue shark, in common with other fish, swims by moving its tail from side to side. Dolphins and whales, on the other hand, move theirs up and down.*

of a pod will work together to try to separate a calf from its mother. Once this has been achieved, they take turns riding up on the calf's back to prevent it reaching the surface to breathe. Transients also hunt down and kill other dolphins.

Smaller than killer whales but still capable of reaching 20 feet (6m) long, pilot whales are social hunters of squid and fish. There are two species, separated by latitude: short-finned pilot whales prefer tropical and subtropical waters; long-finned pilot whales inhabit temperate and sub-polar waters in both hemispheres.

Unlike the majority of dolphins, pilot whales travel relatively slowly and spend many of their daylight hours resting at the surface. This behaviour is known as logging, since from a distance they resemble nothing more than floating logs. Pilot whales feed mainly at night, when the squid they prefer rise from the depths to hunt nearer the surface.

Previous pages: Bottlenose dolphins leap alongside a boat out at sea. Many types of dolphin are attracted to boats and ships, riding in their bow waves or the waves thrown off from their sides.

Above: Squid are active hunters that use their highly developed eyes to locate prey.

Right: A killer whale swims with her young calf. Newborn calves weigh up to 400lb (180kg).

Chapter 4
The Deep

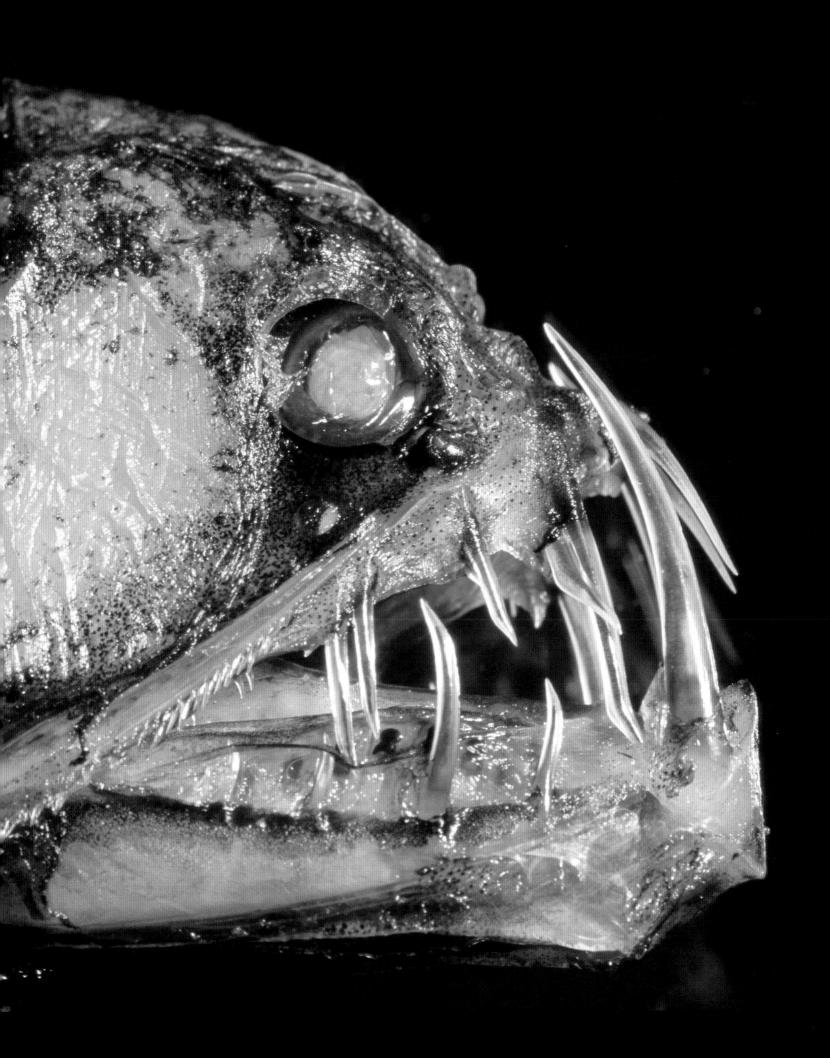

Open water

T he sunlit waters of the sea form a thin layer on its surface. As depth increases, light quickly disappears. Water acts like a filter, absorbing the different wavelengths and colours that make up white light one by one. The first to go is red, soon followed by orange and yellow. Greens and blues penetrate farther before they too are finally completely absorbed. Below 650 feet (198m) no light penetrates at all.

The type of light that filters down through the surface waters affects the colours of the creatures that live there. In the so-called twilight zone, where only blue light penetrates, many creatures are red. The fact that red light does not reach this far down effectively renders them invisible to the other animals around them. Here, being bright red is perfect camouflage and a great way to avoid predators.

Red pigment also absorbs blue light extremely well, enabling red seaweeds and other red algae to survive at much greater depths than their green counterparts. Green algae use the green pigment chlorophyll to capture the light they need for photosynthesis, the process by which they produce their food. Chlorophyll is very good at absorbing red light but not so good at absorbing blue. By using the red pigment phycoerythrin for photosynthesis instead, red algae have a distinct advantage at depth and dominate marine habitats below 100 feet (30m). However, even they cannot survive where there is no light at all and below around 650 feet (198m) they disappear from even the clearest waters.

Light disappears with depth but pressure increases. Pressure is commonly measured in atmospheres. At the sea's surface, the pressure on an object, caused by the weight of the air above it, is exactly one atmosphere. Just 33 feet(10m) below the surface, that pressure is doubled. Another

atmosphere is added with every further 33 feet (10m) of depth. This means that near the bottoms of the deepest ocean trenches, the pressure may be over 1000 atmospheres, the equivalent of more than 7 tons per square inch (10,000 tonnes per square metre).

How do deep sea animals survive these immense pressures? The answer, for most, is simple. They maintain internal pressures that are equal to those of the water outside. This does not involve any special body mechanisms or other trickery, it happens naturally. The fact is that most animals are largely composed of water. In fish and marine invertebrates the water pressure inside their bodies equalizes with that outside since water passes, in a controlled manner, through their body surfaces.

Some fish have gas-filled swim bladders, which they use to control their height in the water column. The gases inside these swim bladders are hugely compressed at depth. This does not normally cause the fish any problems, but if they find themselves suddenly hauled up from the depths the gases expand rapidly as the pressure around them drops. The end result is that the swim bladders balloon out and may even explode.

Page 184: The nautilus spends the day in deep water. As night falls, it rises up the slopes of seamounts to hunt nearer the surface.

Page 185: Lanternfish are among the most common fish in deep water. Like many deep sea creatures, they produce their own light. Each species has its own particular pattern of light organs, which suggests that they use them to help recognize others of their own kind.

Below: The flashlight fish has a pocket beneath each eye which contains glowing bacteria.

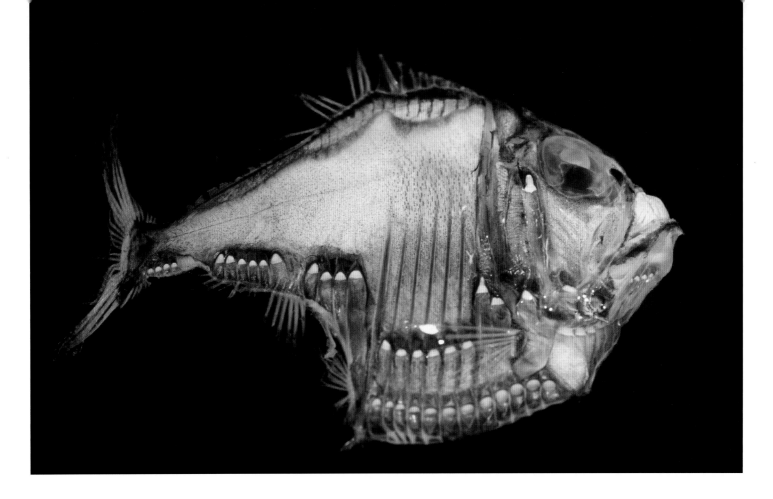

The open water of the deep sea proper, below the twilight zone, is an immense three-dimensional habitat that we on land find hard to comprehend. It covers well over half of the Earth's surface to an average depth of about two miles (3.2km). In many ways it is akin to the air between the land and clouds, at least in its dimensions. Like the air, it is free from physical obstructions to movement. Unlike it, however, it is pitch black and full of living things.

Life in the open water of the deep sea depends ultimately on what comes from above. With no light for photosynthesis there is no phytoplankton. Most of the zooplankton that lives here migrates up through the water column at night to feed on the phytoplankton living near the surface. As dawn approaches, it starts to head back down to the relative safety and darkness of deeper waters where there are fewer filter feeders and small hunters cannot find it by sight.

Other deep-water creatures feed on marine snow, tiny pieces of dead tissue and other organic matter that slowly drift down from above. Many species of zooplankton live almost entirely on this, particularly in deeper water where the distances involved make the migration to feed on phytoplankton impractical. They in turn provide food for larger creatures, such as prawns and small fish.

Some fish make the nightly journey up to surface waters with the zooplankton. One example is the hatchet fish, so named because of the shape of its body. The hatchet fish, like many deep sea creatures, produces light of its own, a phenomenon known as bioluminescence. Perhaps surprisingly, it uses this for camouflage. Rows of light-producing organs on its underside work to make it invisible to predators looking up at it from below. The colour and intensity of light the fish produces exactly matches

Above: *Hatchetfish have rows of light-emitting organs along their undersides. The bodies of these fish are flattened, making them harder to see from above or below.*

that filtering down from above. In the darkness of the deep the hatchet fish has no need of this camouflage but nearer the surface, particularly on moonlit nights, it uses it to reduce the risk of being seen.

Other fish use light to attract prey rather than to avoid predators. Many open-water anglerfish carry a luminescent lure on the end of a living rod, a modified fin ray at the front of the head. This lure is dangled in front of the angler fish's enormous jaws and twitched every so often to make it look like a small, moving animal. Any fish or other creature fooled by this and drawn in by the lure is snapped up and swallowed. Anglerfish, like many deep-sea predators, have highly distensible stomachs, allowing them to ingest prey almost as large as themselves. This is an important aid to survival in a habitat where prey is often scarce and always difficult to locate. Predators cannot afford to miss meals because they are too large to swallow.

Like anglerfish, gulper eels have enormous mouths and stomachs that can expand in size many times over. Although their ribbon-like bodies are rarely more than two feet (60cm) long, their jaws are so large that, fully open, they could swallow a basketball. Some gulper eels also use bioluminescence in a similar way to anglerfish, the main difference being that their lures are attached to their tails. The tail lure is twitched to attract prey into range.

Bioluminescence is produced by a chemical reaction in which a protein called a luciferin is broken down by the addition of oxygen. As the luciferin molecules are destroyed, light is generated. Most animals that use bioluminescence create their own light, but some hijack other organisms to do it for them. The flashlight fish from the Indian Ocean, for example, keeps naturally bioluminescent bacteria in pouches beneath its eyes. These bacteria glow continuously but the flashlight fish is able to switch its lights on and off by opening and closing shutters over the pouches, like eyelids.

The flashlight fish uses its bioluminescence both to attract small animals and to help it see its prey. It shades its lights at the slightest hint of danger, disappearing suddenly from the view of approaching predators.

Other deep-sea creatures produce bioluminescent 'smoke screens' to help them get away. There are species of shrimp and squid that both do this, having evolved the mechanism separately. When they find themselves under attack, they fill the water with bioluminescent material, dazzling would-be predators just long enough for them to make their escape.

The vast majority of creatures that bioluminesce produce light at the blue end of the spectrum. There are two reasons why they do this. Firstly, blue light travels farther through water than light of other colours and secondly, most deep-sea creatures have eyes that are only sensitive to blue or green light. Producing light of any other colour to lure prey would be a waste of time. That said, there is one group of fish, the loosejaws, that generate and can see red light. They have organs just below each eye that shine red light out in front of them, allowing them to spot prey without alerting it to their own presence.

Loosejaws have another feature much more common among deep-sea predatory fish – long, sharp, backward-pointing teeth. These give them a better than average chance of snagging prey and ensure that, once caught, it does not escape.

Perhaps the most spectacular teeth of any deep sea creatures belong to the viperfish. These eel-like predators have long fangs that stick out from their jaws by necessity: if they did not, the fish would be unable to close their mouths. Viperfish also have another striking adaptation, one to prevent themselves becoming prey. Their stomachs are covered by an extra-dark lining of tissue which works like a curtain, shielding the light produced by any bioluminescent creatures that they might eat.

Although they look terrifying, viperfish are quite small, rarely exceeding a foot (30cm) in length. They are closely related to another group of even smaller and much more innocuous open-water fish, the bristlemouths. These little-known plankton feeders grow to just three inches (7.6cm) long and are thought to be the most abundant fish in the sea. Like hatchet fish, they have rows of light-producing organs along their bellies to camouflage them against light filtering down from above at night, when they swim up near to the surface to feed.

Previous pages: Some anglerfish live in open water but others lie in wait for prey on the seabed. Bottom-dwelling anglerfish, like this species, are also known as monkfish, and are prized for their flesh.

Below: With their long fangs and snake-like bodies, viperfish are well named. In common with those of many other deep-sea fish, their stomachs are extremely elastic, enabling them to take full advantage of rare gluts of food.

Many types of squid generate their own light too. After fish, squid are the most common predatory creatures of any real size in the deep sea. Most bioluminescent squid generate light for camouflage, like bristle-mouths and hatchet fish. Some change the colour of the light they produce depending on the temperature of the water. When they feel cold, they give off a faint blue light, but as they warm up they change their colour to green. This temperature-dependent system is not as strange as it might at first seem. Deeper water is colder than shallow and these squid migrate up with the plankton at night. In the shallows near the surface more green light penetrates the water, so it makes sense to be green. By day, the squid cruise down to the edge of the twilight zone where the water is colder and only blue light reaches.

Not all squid produce light for camouflage; some do it to escape pred-ators. As has already been mentioned, several species squirt out clouds of bioluminescent ink when in danger. Others flash light organs suddenly to startle attackers. One squid that does this grows to seven feet (2m) long. Known as *Taningia danae* it lives at depths down to 3000 feet (914m) in most of the world's oceans. *Taningia danae* has the largest known light-producing organs of any animal, two gigantic yellow photophores held like light bulbs, one on the end of each of its longest arms. When it comes under attack, it flashes these suddenly, stopping many predators in their tracks. Like the flashlight fish, it switches its lights on and off by means of an eyelid-like membrane, which can be opened and closed at will.

Above: *The eye-flash squid is found at depths of more than 2600 feet (800m) during daylight hours, but at night it migrates to warmer surface waters. It is able to change the colour of its bioluminescence according to the temperature of the water, which aids camouflage in both sunlight and moonlight.*

Taningia danae is a large squid but it is by no means the largest in the sea. That title is shared by two true monsters, the giant squid and the less well-known colossal squid. Scientists currently disagree over which is the bigger of the two – the fact that few living specimens of either species have ever been seen compounds the argument. What is known is that both are absolutely enormous, far bigger than any other invertebrates known to exist.

The giant squid lives in the depths of most of the world's oceans and was recently photographed for the first time, using a camera dropped on a baited line to around 3000 feet (914m). The pictures, taken by a Japanese research team in September 2005, showed it to be an active predator. How it finds its prey in the total darkness at this depth remains a mystery, although it seems likely that smell might play a part. The fact that the individual photographed found the bait – a dead fish hanging still on the end of a line – suggests that, in this case at least, the squid was not hunting by picking up vibrations from movement in the water.

Higher up, in the twilight zone, the giant squid almost certainly uses eyesight to track and catch its prey. This species has the largest eyes of any animal, up to a foot (30cm) across. Like all cephalopod molluscs (squid, octopuses and cuttlefish) its eyes are extremely well developed and have many physical similarities to our own, including a muscular 'iris', to regulate the amount of light entering, and a hard lens to focus images. Many cephalopods can see in full colour, although it seems unlikely that the giant squid can do so, given that it spends most of its life in darkness or bathed only by the faintest blue light.

The colossal squid is even more mysterious than the giant squid, partly because it seems only to inhabit deep waters in polar and subpolar

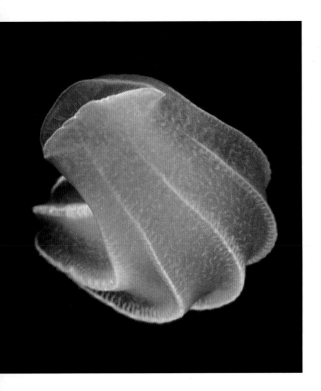

Left: *Most of the 90 or so known species of comb jelly inhabit surface waters but some, such as this one, are deep-sea creatures, living as much as 10,000 feet (3280m) down.*

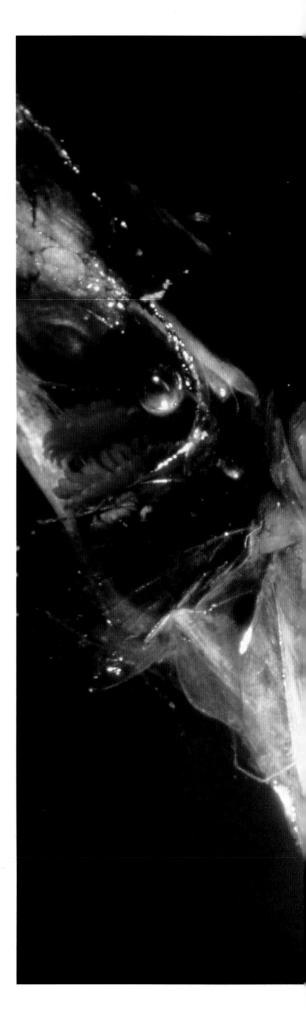

Right: *The tube-eye or thread-tail hangs in the water column, waiting for free-swimming crustaceans and other small prey to swim past. When it spots a potential meal glowing or silhouetted against the distant surface, it expands the huge pouch below its lower jaw to suck it into its mouth.*

seas. What is known is that its two longest arms end in clubs covered with fearsome, swivelling hooks. Like the giant squid, its arms also have large circular suckers to grab on to prey, which it pulls towards its mouth containing a huge beak not unlike that of a parrot.

Sightings of intact giant and colossal squid, alive or dead, are exceedingly rare. Most of what is known of them, including their size (both are thought to attain lengths of 60 feet/18m or more), comes from body parts recovered from the stomachs of their principal predator, the sperm whale.

Sperm whales are the world's greatest deep sea divers. Like all mammals, they must breathe air, yet they hunt prey well over a mile (1.6km) beneath the surface. Individual dives may last for as much as two hours. Sperm whales achieve these incredible feats with the aid of some unique physical adaptations. Before each dive they lie for some time at the surface breathing deeply. This not only fills their lungs but also gives their bodies time for the blood to stock up all the muscles and other body tissues with oxygen. During shorter, shallower dives only the oxygen in the lungs is used, but when they dive at depth the lungs collapse and the oxygen stored in their body tissues comes into play. Other physiological changes reduce the amount of oxygen used: the heartbeat slows right down, for example, and oxygen is channelled only to the areas that need it most, such as the brain.

Sperm whales find their prey in the darkness by using echolocation. The spermaceti organ, a huge cavity in the head filled with yellowy wax, helps to focus the loud clicks these whales make into a sonic beam. The echoes that bounce back off squid give their positions away and lead the whales to them.

Sperm whales are the fifth largest animals on Earth and the biggest of all the planet's active predators. A fully grown bull sperm whale can be as much as 60 feet (18m) long and weigh over 50 tons/tonnes.

Two much smaller whales share a similar lifestyle. The pygmy sperm whale and the dwarf sperm whale are only distantly related to their giant namesake but have evolved a similar appearance due to the fact that they hunt the same sort of prey, deep water squid. Both are poorly understood and rarely observed in the wild. The dwarf sperm whale is the smallest of all the true whales, being shorter and weighing less than a bottlenose dolphin. It is thought to dive to depths of at least 1000 feet (305m).

The sheer vastness of the open ocean and the deep sea is brought home when one considers the beaked whales. There are 20 species of beaked whale altogether, yet many of these are known only from rare strandings and have never been seen alive in the wild. Beaked whales are great divers and most feed on squid. They range in size from 11 feet to 31 feet (3.3m to 9.4m) long and are thought to be distributed throughout the world's oceans, with different species concentrated in particular areas. In most species, the females have no teeth at all. Males have two or four large teeth, which erupt from the lower jaw.

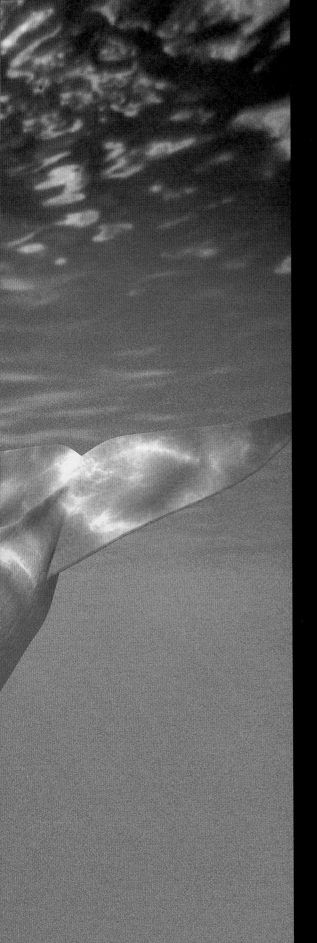

Previous pages: This extremely rare picture shows a Blainville's beaked whale in waters near Hawaii. Beaked whales feed at great depths but they are rarely seen and very little is known about the details of their lives. Like all whales, they must return to the surface to breathe.

Left: The sperm whale is the world's largest predator. It feeds mainly on giant squid, which it hunts in complete darkness far below the ocean's surface.

Above: Humboldt squid can grow up to 6 feet (1.8m) long. They spend most of their time at depths of 650 to 2300 feet (198 to 700m) but are occasionally seen near the surface at night.

The deep seabed

More than a mile (1.6km) down, the bottom of the sea is like another world. Here vast plains, plunging trenches and sheer-sided mountains all lie cloaked in total darkness. Much of this hidden landscape, comprising the majority of the Earth's crust, is uncharted. Most of it is utterly silent and cold.

Incredibly, life actually flourishes here. Far from the warming rays of the sun and subject to crushing pressures that would cause our fragile bodies to implode, countless animals go about their lives, as oblivious to the world above as we normally are to them.

Although some of the creatures that live here look vaguely familiar, others are completely bizarre. Some are throwbacks from distant eras in our planet's past, living fossils preserved unchanged in an environment that itself has barely altered in hundreds of millions of years.

One such creature is the coelacanth. A century ago it was known only from fossils formed in rocks more than 70 million years old.

Then, in 1938, one was pulled up from the deep sea off the shores of South Africa. The coelacanth is a lobe-finned fish, a living member of the group that gave rise to the first vertebrates to walk on land. The bases of its fins contain bones that resemble those found in the earliest precursors of legs. It may use them, scientists think, to prop itself up on the seabed.

The coelacanth is the most famous living fossil to be recovered from the deep sea but there are many other primitive forms of fish that still inhabit this environment. Hagfish are deep-sea scavengers that scour the seabed for the bodies of dead animals that fall down from above. Together with lampreys, they comprise the jawless fish, the most primitive of all fish alive today. As the name suggests, these creatures have no jaws but

instead have mouths like suckers, lined with circles of small, sharp teeth. They use these to attach themselves to the flesh of dead animals, tying their flexible, eel-like bodies in knots to rip chunks away. Hagfish find their food in the darkness using their keen sense of smell. They will consume flesh that is weeks or even months old, slithering through the skeletons of carcasses until every bone is picked clean.

The deep sea is also home to the world's most ancient sharks. Sharks as a group are quite primitive, having evolved before bony fish, which now dominate the oceans in terms of species. But some sharks are more primitive than others. Those that have changed least since the group first appeared 420 million years ago are the six-gilled and seven-gilled sharks. These lack the large front dorsal fin characteristic of most sharks.

Six-gilled and seven-gilled sharks are slow swimmers that tend to hug the seabed in search of carrion and unsuspecting prey. In common with other sharks, they have an extremely good sense of smell, which leads them towards food in the darkness of the deep. Other deep-water sharks include the bizarre-looking goblin shark, a sluggish hunter of seabed invertebrates and small fish. The goblin shark has a very long and flattened snout, which protrudes from the front of its head like some sort of fleshy shelf. Its mouth adds to its freakish appearance. Unlike most sharks which have their jaws neatly hidden beneath the smooth surfaces

Page 198: The Japanese spider crab has a leg span of some 12 feet (3.6m). Like many of the deep-sea bottom dwellers, it is a scavenger.

Page 199: The Johnson Sea Link research submersible begins a dive near the Bahamas. Equipped with cameras, lights and a robotic arm linked to a suction tube, it can both record and collect specimens from the deep sea.

Below: Hagfish are among the most primitive fish in the sea. They feed almost entirely on carrion, twisting themselves into knots to rip off chunks from dead animals lying on the sea floor.

of their bodies, the goblin shark has jaws that stick out some distance from the underside of its head. It is thought that it may use these to rummage through the material of the seabed itself as it searches for food. Despite the fact that it feeds on relatively small prey, the goblin shark can reach more than 10 feet (3m) long.

Many other species of shark live near the seabed but feed in open water. Among them are the lantern sharks, so named because their bodies secrete a luminous slime which covers their skin. Lantern sharks are small and poorly understood, although one species, the green lantern shark, has been better studied than most. The green lantern shark is notable because of its unusual behaviour. Unlike most sharks, it appears to hunt in packs. Green lantern sharks grow to just 10 inches (25.4cm) long, making them among the smallest of all shark species. However, they hunt deep-sea squid substantially larger than themselves, harrying their prey in groups and gradually wearing it down.

A close relative of the green lantern shark is the somewhat larger cookie cutter. It feeds on a variety of large animals, including the biggest deep-sea creature of all, the sperm whale. The cookie cutter does not kill its prey but rather takes bite-sized chunks out of its skin. Fully open, its mouth forms an almost perfect circle, lined with sharp-edged teeth. It uses this to clamp on to its prey and then twists its body to tear off a mouthful of flesh. The circular wounds it leaves are what give this five-foot (1.5m) long species its name. Cookie cutters have been known to

Above: *Frogfish are close relatives of anglerfish and, like them, use lures attached to a spine which they wave to attract prey. Many frogfish are extremely well camouflaged and can lie completely still for hours as they wait for prey to come within reach.*

Following pages: *The coelacanth was originally known only from fossils and caused a sensation when it was found to still be living in the Indian Ocean. This ancient creature has barely changed for 400 million years. It belongs to the lobe-finned group of fish, which biologists believe gave rise to the amphibians, the first vertebrates to live on land.*

attack the audio reception cables on the outside of research submarines and sometimes destroy undersea telephone lines. It is thought that they are drawn to the electric fields these produce. Most sharks are able to detect the electrical pulses given off by the muscles of their prey and they probably mistake these man-made electric fields for signs of food.

One of the largest and weirdest-looking of all deep-sea sharks only came to light in 1976. Even then, its discovery was an accident – it was hauled up off Hawaii after becoming entangled in an anchor chain. Since then, two more specimens of this species, now known as the megamouth shark, have been recovered. Growing to 14 feet (4.2m) long, it is a filter feeder that lives on plankton like the basking shark and whale shark, which both inhabit shallower waters. It is so different from these and other sharks, however, that it has been given a new family of its own in animal classification.

The megamouth shark is aptly named – like most filter feeders it has an enormous gape to maximize the amount of food entering its body as it swims through the water. Examination of its stomach contents has shown that it often swallows small squid as well as plankton and other less mobile creatures such as jellyfish. These may actually be drawn towards it and into its gaping maw as it cruises along. The inside of its mouth is covered with numerous tiny luminous organs, which may act as lures to tempt in squid and other small prey.

A huge range of other weird fish inhabit the deep seabed. Among them are the ratfish, distant relatives of the sharks and rays. Like rays, ratfish move by undulating their pectoral fins. Their long, streamer-like tails are useless for propulsion but trail out behind as they swim slowly just above the seabed. Ratfish feed mainly on crabs and other shellfish, crushing their meals between their plate-like teeth. Although, like sharks and rays, they have skeletons made of cartilage, they also have many features in common with bony fish, leading scientists to believe that they might represent an evolutionary link between the two groups.

Many deep-sea rays have similar diets and habits to ratfish, although they also use their electro-receptive sense to find prey hidden beneath the seabed sand and mud. Bony flatfish, such as megrim and halibut, also inhabit this environment. They feed mainly on smaller bottom-dwelling fish that blunder into range.

The deep-sea floor is home to many kinds of fish but invertebrates (creatures without backbones) are far more common. Echinoderms are particularly abundant. This invertebrate group is made up almost entirely of animals that, as adults, cannot swim, specifically the starfish, feather stars, sea lilies, sea urchins and sea cucumbers.

In some parts of the ocean feather stars almost completely cover the seabed. They are particularly common on the abyssal plains, great stretches of almost featureless terrain a mile (1.6km) or more below the surface. Feather stars are named for their many bristled arms, which

resemble feathers. They use these to capture falling particles of marine snow, intercepting it just before it reaches the seabed. They also capture and eat planktonic animals. Feather stars are able to move, albeit slowly, but they do not use their feathery arms for locomotion. Instead, they use much smaller legs hidden beneath.

Sea lilies are very closely related to feather stars and feed in exactly the same way. The main difference between the two is that sea lilies spend their adult lives attached to one spot, held in place by a flexible 'stalk'. This gives them the appearance of submarine flowers, hence their name.

Sea urchins have protective, mobile spines and move slowly over the seabed by means of these and their many tube feet. Deep-sea species feed on carrion and other organic matter on the sea floor. They find their food by tasting the water and following the trails of particles suspended within it.

Most sea cucumbers are a little bit like gigantic earthworms in the way that they feed, but they live on the seabed rather than in it. They move slowly along, sucking up the sediment of the seabed as they go. Any organic matter within it is digested and the rest is expelled. Sea cucumbers, like all echinoderms, have hard plates of calcite embedded in their skin. This is enough to make them unpalatable to most creatures but they also have a second line of defence. If harassed, they fire threads of sticky material from their anus, which are sufficient to disable most small predators and distract or put off larger ones.

Starfish feed both on carrion and living prey. There are more than 1800 species known to science so far and doubtless countless others waiting to be discovered in the depths of the sea. Many starfish prey on bivalve molluscs, such as scallops, which they find on the seabed. They grab hold of these using the many tiny suction pads on their tube feet and slowly pull their prey's hinged shells apart. Once they have opened a gap wide enough, they eject their stomach and slowly force it in to digest the flesh inside. The whole process may take hours or even days,

Brittle stars resemble starfish but have much more flexible arms. These enable them to move relatively quickly over the seabed. Most feed on carrion and organic detritus but some hunt small worms and crustaceans. A few are filter feeders like the feather stars, sifting plankton and other particles of food from the water.

Like the echinoderms, lobsters, crabs, prawns and other crustaceans inhabit the floor of the deep sea in huge numbers, most picking through the bodies of dead animals that rain down from above. Some deep-sea crustaceans grow to incredible sizes. The heaviest known species is the North Atlantic lobster, which can reach 44 pounds (20kg) – more than the average 5-year-old child. Although not quite as weighty, some crabs grow even larger, at least in terms of leg span. The biggest of all, as far as we know, is the Japanese spider crab, which has a leg span of more than 12 feet (3.6m). It is thought to live for as long as 100 years.

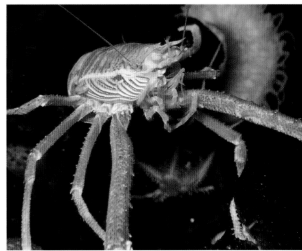

Above: The squat lobster is actually a type of crab which lives on sand and mud seabeds at depths of over 4000 feet (1200m). These small crustaceans can actively swim in deep water and they feed on carrion and small plankton.

While most squid inhabit open water, their close cousins the octopuses hug the sea floor. Deep-sea octopuses include some truly weird-looking animals. One recently discovered species has acquired the nickname 'Dumbo' because it moves through the water by flapping appendages that look like giant ears. Octopuses are predators that hunt crustaceans and fish. Unlike squid, which shoal, they tend to spend most of their time alone, only seeking out others of their own kind to breed.

The majority of deep-sea octopuses are relatively small but one species grows to well over 12 feet (3.6m) long. One specimen of this creature, which currently goes only by the scientific name *Haliphron atlanticus*, was trawled up off New Zealand in 2001. Despite missing half of its tentacles, its remains were found to weigh just under 135 pounds (61kg).

Generally speaking, the deep-sea floor is dark, cold and silent, its creatures ultimately dependent on food generated in the sunlit waters above. There are a few places, however, where things are very different. Here, whole ecosystems flourish without any energy from sunlight at all.

On the mid-ocean ridges, where immense forces slowly drag plates of the Earth's crust apart, molten rock surges up to fill the gaps. Under the immense pressure, this heats the water to scalding temperatures, far higher than those at which it would boil in air. In places, this superheated water, filled with dissolved minerals, shoots out from submarine geysers known as black smokers.

Black smokers support unique communities of primitive bacteria, which absorb the minerals and use them to produce the nutrients they need to survive. These bacteria form the basis of self-contained food chains, comprising species of animals found nowhere else in the sea. Giant tube worms flourish on the sides of the geyser 'chimneys', where the water is still so hot that it would kill most other creatures. Unlike their smaller filter-feeding relatives elsewhere in the sea they survive on nutrients produced by primitive bacteria, which live symbiotically within their body tissues. Other simple invertebrates here include clams and mussels which do filter feed but also rely partly on symbiotic bacteria living inside them.

So far, more than 300 different species of animals have been found living on and around black smokers, ranging from small prawns and crabs to eel-like fish. The inaccessibility of these habitats means that they have only begun to be explored by unmanned submersibles, and there are doubtless many more strange and unique animals living among them still waiting to be discovered.

Black smokers were first found by deep-sea researchers in 1977. Their existence had been predicted by some but the communities of life they supported came as a great surprise. In 1990, another deep-sea habitat was discovered that no one had expected to find. In the Gulf of Mexico, a mile (1.6km) below the surface, roving submersibles stumbled across what appeared to be a lake on the seabed. Closer examination revealed that it was made up of superconcentrated brine. Like a lake on land, it had

Below: *Black smokers form around areas of volcanic activity on the seabed. Sea water which enters cracks in the rock is super-heated then expelled from underwater geysers, loaded with dissolved minerals. Because of the pressures under which this happens, the water reaches temperatures far higher than boiling point on land. Around the edges of these smokers, where temperatures are more bearable, life thrives.*

shores and gentle ripples on its surface. However, rather than birds or dragonflies skimming over it, there were fish.

The lake's shores were encrusted with thousands of mussels and nearby there were large beds of tube worms. All of these creatures were existing without the sun's energy. Like the black smokers, it transpired, this ecosystem was built on bacteria able to generate food from sulphides, a sort of submarine alternative to photosynthesis. Although this is the only such lake discovered so far, many more are thought likely to exist in the unexplored vastness of the deep seabed.

Left: Most dives to the deep seabed are made by unmanned submersibles. These are controlled remotely from the surface. Here, a technician operates a deep-sea submersible from the control room on board the research vessel Thompson G. Thompson exploring in the Pacific Ocean.

Top: Many species of octopus hunt on the deep sea floor. This one was photographed using lights in the North Atlantic Ocean.

Above: Some deep-sea creatures look like they might have come from another planet. This sea cucumber lives in deep waters off Canada's Arctic coast.

Chapter 5
Polar Seas

Cold Comfort

The Arctic and Southern Oceans are tough places to live but reward creatures that can survive in them. Their waters are among the most productive on Earth. In summer they receive sunlight 24 hours a day, allowing microscopic algae and other phytoplankton to bloom. These in turn feed huge numbers of crustaceans and fish, which draw in predators great and small, and support massive breeding colonies of marine mammals and sea birds.

In winter the polar oceans' bounty is locked away. Although their waters are still rich with nutrients, the sun disappears for months at a time, meaning that those nutrients cannot be harnessed. The green plankton, which rely on sunlight to drive the process of photosynthesis and make food, shut down production and wait for the spring. Most of those that are not eaten die back, with just enough remaining to keep the water's few animal residents ticking over. The majority of creatures that able to leave for warmer climes do so. Only when the sun comes back do they begin to return.

Even in the summer, polar waters are bitterly cold and many areas are encrusted with ice. In the Arctic Ocean a permanent ice cap floats on top of the sea, surrounded by floes of broken ice. The North Pole itself is not on land but water, albeit frozen.

The South Pole by contrast is on land, the southerly continent of Antarctica. In winter, this huge land mass is completely covered by ice and snow. Even in the height of summer, bare rock is only exposed at its fringes. The Antarctic ice cap extends out over the sea, forming a permanent cover in some places but a seasonal one in others. As in the Arctic, it is bordered by pack ice and icebergs.

Many polar creatures spend much of their time out on the ice, resting between meals or raising their young. Their abundance in these frozen wastes is testament to the richness of the waters below and to the capacity of life to adapt and flourish in even the most extreme conditions.

Right: *A leopard seal rests on ice in Antarctica's Paradise Bay. Leopard seals are formidable hunters, counting other seals among their prey.*

Above it all

In summer, the skies over polar waters are filled with sea birds. Huge numbers migrate to arrive in spring and breed, taking advantage of the seasonal bounty to feed and raise their chicks.

In the Arctic, the birds nest on islands and the northerly coastlines of Alaska, Canada, Greenland, Norway and Russia. In winter most of these places are hidden beneath snow and ice, but, for a few brief months in spring and summer, average temperatures rise high enough to free them from its grip. Cliffs are quickly colonized by thick-billed murres and black guillemots. Tufted puffins dig burrows in cliff-top soil, while little auks, or dovekies, nest among the rocks and boulders on steep slopes inland. All of these birds feed on small fish and crustaceans at sea, drifting on the waves in great rafts and diving from the surface to catch their prey under-water. With their short, stubby wings they are poor fliers, but they flap through water with a grace only surpassed by penguins. Black guillemots, the deepest divers, may 'fly' down to depths of 600 feet (182m) in pursuit of prey. As well as feeding themselves, they have to feed their chicks, and parents make frequent trips between their nests and the sea.

Other Arctic sea birds are less adept at hunting for themselves but very good at stealing the catches of others. Arctic skuas are like the frigate birds of the north, harrying smaller species in the air and forcing them to drop or disgorge their prey. In some parts of their range these birds are known as parasitic jaegers, but wherever they breed, they nest a little way inland, preferring dry tundra or rocky uplands. Unlike the species they bully for food, Arctic skua pairs nest away from others of their own kind. They defend their eggs and young aggressively, dive-bombing any animal that wanders too close.

Perhaps surprisingly, the waters of the Arctic Ocean are home to ducks. Eiders, king eiders and oldsquaws spend most of their time at sea feeding on small crustaceans and only come ashore to breed. All three of these ducks are consummate divers, searching for prey both in open water and on the bottom close to shore. Eiders are famous for the quality of their downy feathers, which they use to line their nests. This eider-down is the same as that used to fill quilts and pillows. It is collected after the ducklings have fledged and left their nests.

Gulls are to be found along most of the world's coasts and those of the Arctic are no exception. Glaucous and Iceland gulls are among the larger species. Like most gulls, they are opportunistic, feeding on everything from fish to carrion. They also raid the nests of other birds, stealing unguarded eggs and young chicks. Ivory gulls are more dainty and, as their name suggests, completely white, apart from their bills, legs and feet. Black-legged kittiwakes are unusual among gulls in two respects: firstly, they breed in dense colonies crowded on to cliffs and secondly, they often feed far from shore, picking planktonic crustaceans and young Arctic cod from the surface, usually while in flight.

Page 214: A black guillemot returns from a successful fishing trip.

Page 215: Tufted puffins perch on a coastal ledge in Alaska, overlooking the Bering Sea. Like the common puffins of Europe, tufted puffins nest in holes which they dig at the tops of cliffs.

Opposite: An ivory gull picks at the scraps of a larger animal's meal. Ivory gulls have been known to follow polar bears for weeks in the high Arctic, living off their left-overs.

Below: An Arctic skua stands over her eggs, laid directly on the ground. Arctic skuas raid the nests of other birds and are more than capable of defending their own eggs from most predators.

Terns are often confused with gulls but apart from their size and general colouration the two groups are quite different. Terns are far more graceful fliers and catch their food – small fish and other surface water creatures – by diving at it from the air. They also have narrower, more pointed bills than gulls and longer tails, which are often forked. The Arctic tern is a classic polar species. In fact, in many ways it is the ultimate polar bird. It arrives in the Arctic to breed in May or June, then leaves a few months later to make its way to the other end of the Earth. It spends the southern summer at sea in the waters off Antarctica. Some Arctic terns clock up more than 20,000 miles (32,186km) a year with their migrations, which are by far the longest undertaken by any bird.

Arctic terns are unusual in arriving during the Antarctic summer just to feed. Most birds, which make much shorter migrations from elsewhere in the Southern Hemisphere, come to nest and raise their young. Albatrosses are just one example. When they are not breeding, these huge sea birds spend their lives out over open water, gliding on the updrafts that form over the crests of waves. They feed on fish and squid, which they catch at the surface, and travel vast distances in search of prey. The largest species, the wandering and royal albatrosses, often fly right around the Southern Ocean, riding the prevailing winds.

Most albatrosses mate for life and breed once every two years. Once partners have reunited and built their mound-shaped nest, the female lays a single egg. Albatross chicks take several months to fledge and at first are guarded by one parent while the other forages at sea. Only when they are large enough to fend off attacks from other sea birds are the chicks left alone, permitting both parents to search for food at the same time and bring back more for the growing youngster.

Albatrosses prefer to nest on sub-Antarctic islands a little way north of the pack ice but there are flying birds that nest on the continent itself. Like their Arctic counterparts, Antarctic skuas bully other sea birds to force them to regurgitate their prey. They also feed on unguarded penguin eggs and chicks, and are a common sight around most penguin colonies. Antarctic skuas are great fliers and often nest a long way from the sea. They are occasionally sighted hundreds of miles inland, flying over otherwise barren expanses of ice.

The Antarctic skua is quite a large bird but it is dwarfed by the continent's other main winged predator, the giant petrel. This fearsome-looking bird has a seven foot (2m) wingspan and is armed with a massive hooked bill for tearing through flesh. As well as hunting, giant petrels often feed on carrion. A dead seal or whale will attract them like vultures from miles around.

Other Antarctic petrels are smaller and some could even be described as dainty. The Cape petrel, for instance, is about the size of a pigeon and has a small, neat bill for hunting krill and squid. Sitting on their exposed, rocky nests in their dapper plumage Cape petrels look thoroughly

innocuous. However, their appearance is deceptive. If approached, they regurgitate a jet of foul-smelling oil from their stomachs, sometimes firing it several feet.

The snow petrel and Antarctic fulmar both use the same defence mechanism as the Cape petrel. The snow petrel is entirely white, apart from its bill and feet, and nests in crevices between rocks. The Antarctic fulmar, like its northerly namesake (which it resembles) nests on cliffs. They share the continent with one other species of petrel, the storm petrel, which is mainly active at night. This tiny bird is not much bigger than a sparrow but spends most of its life out over the open ocean, where it feeds. As its name suggests, it is a fearless flier, often seen on the wing in the most horrendous gales. Although it breeds on Antarctica, it also nests in many other parts of the world. Some scientists believe that it may be the planet's most common wild bird, with as many as a billion individuals distributed across the planet.

One other flying bird breeds on Antarctica, the sheathbill. Unusually, considering where it lives, it does not have webbed feet and generally avoids the water, spending most of its time on the ice instead. The sheathbill has been described as as Antarctica's dustman and it is an appropriate moniker. Almost nothing seems to be too disgusting for it to consider. As well as carrion, it also eats other birds' faeces and so is never short of a meal in the penguin colonies, where it tends to be found.

Previous pages: *The Arctic tern nests in the Arctic but leaves as winter approaches and migrates to the Antarctic to feed. The Arctic tern's globetrotting lifestyle means that it spends a greater proportion of its life in sunlight than any other creature on Earth.*

Above: *Snow petrels are among the few birds to nest inland on the Antarctic continent itself.*

Left: *A wandering albatross greets his mate with a display on South Georgia's aptly named Albatross Island.*

Above: The grey-headed albatross spends most of the year on the open ocean, feeding on squid and fish. In October, it makes its way to the sub-Antarctic islands where it breeds. Once the single egg has been laid, the male does most of the incubation.

Right: Slightly larger than the grey-headed albatross, with a wingspan of up to 8 feet (2.5m), the black-browed albatross has a similar lifestyle and nests on many of the same islands. The black-browed albatross builds its nest from mud. This colony is on the Falkland Islands.

Top: *The south polar skua is a predator that patrols penguin colonies looking for isolated eggs and chicks to eat.*

Above: *Like other albatrosses, the light-mantled sooty albatross appears effortless in flight, riding the wind with its pointed, outstretched wings.*

Right: *The giant petrel might be considered the vulture of the sea. This large, aggressive bird feeds mainly on carrion, although it also hunts and kills the chicks of other sea birds.*

Out in the cold

Many polar creatures treat the ocean like a larder, venturing in to find food but spending much of their time out on the ice. All of these animals are either birds or mammals, air-breathing creatures that have adapted to life in the sea.

The birds most associated with polar wastes are penguins. These flightless fish eaters are found only in the Southern Hemisphere and in many ways are the emblems of the Antarctic. In reality, only four species actually nest on Antarctica itself: the Adélie penguin, the emperor penguin, the chinstrap penguin and the gentoo. All of the other 13 species breed on sub-Antarctic islands or coasts farther north. Two species, for instance, nest on South American shores and one on the southern tip of Africa. There are even penguins that swim in tropical waters just below the equator, around the Galápagos Islands in the Pacific Ocean. Nevertheless, the Southern Ocean and the cold waters bordering it are the penguins' stronghold. Far more of these birds live here than anywhere else in the world.

Penguins are superbly adapted for swimming. Their bodies are smooth and teardrop shaped, enabling them to cut through the water, and their wings have evolved into stiff paddles, with most of the bones inside them fused together for strength. Their feathers are small and all grow towards the feet to minimize resistance in the water. Even their colouration is an adaptation to life in the sea, simple counter-shading which helps to camouflage them from marine predators.

All penguins catch and eat fish when the opportunity arises but some have adapted in body and habit to concentrate on different food. King and emperor penguins, for instance, mainly hunt squid. Their long beaks are

an adaptation to help them grip this soft and slippery prey. Some smaller penguins, such as the Adélie, feed more on krill, shrimp-like crustaceans that swarm in Antarctic waters. Because their favoured prey is found near the surface, they rarely make deep dives. The king and emperor, by contrast, often plunge to significant depths to find their prey. The emperor penguin actually dives deeper than any other bird, sometimes swimming down more than 1000 feet (304m) into the darkness to follow fleeing shoals of squid.

Emperor penguins are perhaps the hardiest creatures on Earth. The males spend the Antarctic winter out on the ice, balancing their partners' eggs on their feet and incubating them beneath a flap of feathery skin. Male emperor penguins huddle together for warmth during these icy months of darkness, enduring screaming gales with winds of 125mph (200km/h) and temperatures as low as -76°F (-60°C). Each takes his turn on the outside of the huddle to ensure that the group as a whole survives. During the entire period that their partners are at sea, two months or more, the male emperor penguins do not feed once. By the time relief finally arrives in the shape of the females, they may have lost half of their body weight.

Page 226: A polar bear stalks across Arctic ice. Out of the water, the polar bear is the Arctic's top predator.

Page 227: Emperor penguins move about on the ice by both by walking and tobogganing along on their bellies.

Above: Chinstrap penguins are among the world's most common, with a population estimated at around 18 million birds.

Right: Emperor penguins incubate their eggs and raise their chicks on the ice sheets extending out from the Antarctic continent.

Emperors are the largest penguins, reaching four feet (1.2m) tall. In fact, they are the biggest of all marine birds. They incubate their eggs through the winter to give their chicks time to grow large enough in the short Antarctic summer to fledge and take to the sea. Smaller penguins do not have the same problem with growth. They, like most other sea birds, nest and lay their eggs in spring.

Even when they do not have eggs or chicks, penguins spend a lot of time out of the water. Around Antarctica, Adélies and chinstraps in particular can often be seen seen riding on icebergs or resting on slabs of floating ice. There is a very good reason for this: their main predators live in the sea. Penguins are often caught by killer whales but they have an even more dedicated predator, the leopard seal.

Leopard seals specialize in hunting penguins. Unlike most seals, which hunt mainly fish or crustaceans, they have very large mouths and particularly fearsome teeth. They lurk in the water at the edge of ice floes, waiting for penguins to return from feeding at sea. Another hunting tactic of theirs is follow the shadows of penguins walking on thin ice then smash their way through. They even sometimes catch penguins out on the ice itself, waiting near the water's edge then grabbing the birds as they emerge from the sea.

Below: The leopard seal's large closed mouth hides a battery of vicious teeth. This Antarctic species preys heavily on penguins, catching them in the water and smashing up through the ice to grab them unawares. Leopard seals are large animals, growing to 10 feet (3.3m) long and weighing a third of a ton/tonne.

Leopard seals are mammals that give birth out on the ice. Most of the time, however, they remain in the water, hunting or waiting for prey.

Other Antarctic seals have different habits. Crabeater seals spend much of their time out of the sea. Despite their name, they feed mainly on krill in the surface waters around the pack ice, which surrounds the Antarctic ice cap proper. When they are not feeding, crabeaters prefer to rest on floating chunks of ice. Here they are relatively safe from their main predators, killer whales, and from leopard seals which often prey on their young. Crabeater seals are by far the most numerous of all the world's seal species and are the most common large animals around Antarctica. Most estimates put their population in excess of 30 million.

Weddell seals, by contrast, are much more at home in the water. They live beneath the fast ice, which forms the floating edge of the Antarctic ice cap itself, out of reach of killer whales and leopard seals. Because air temperatures here are always below freezing, they have to work hard to maintain breathing holes in the ice. Most Weddell seals die not from predation but starvation, their teeth having worn away after years of gnawing away at the ice.

Ross seals live in heavy pack ice where few ships ever venture and little is known of their habits. What is known is that they prefer to feed on squid. Ross seals are large animals, reaching eight feet (2.4m) long. Unusually for mammals, the females are bigger than the males.

The largest of all seals is the southern elephant seal, which feeds in Antarctic waters and breeds on islands both in the Southern Ocean and

Above: Despite its name, the crabeater seal rarely feeds on crabs – its main diet is krill, another type of crustacean. Crabeaters are by far the world's most common seals. Some scientists estimate that there may be as many as 40 million of them alive at any one time – more than the populations of all the world's other seals and sea lions put together.

Following pages: Like the crabeater seal, the Weddell seal lives in Antarctic waters. It is the world's most southerly mammal, living and hunting for fish underneath the Antarctic ice sheet, and surviving by maintaining breathing holes in the ice.

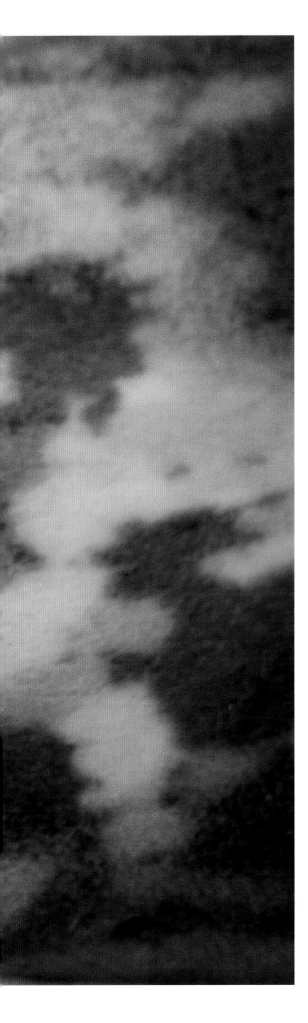

farther north. As with its slightly smaller cousin, the northern elephant seal, there is huge sexual dimorphism in this species. The males are enormous, growing several times larger than the females. The reason for this is selective evolutionary pressure caused by the southern elephant seal's breeding system. Males battle to control whole areas of the beaches on which they breed and the larger, stronger individuals invariably win. These males then mate with all the females on that section of beach and so father the next generation. Their sons carry half of their genes and so are more likely to grow into giants than they would if they had been fathered by smaller males.

Southern elephant seals satisfy their huge appetites with squid and deep-sea fish. They dive deeper than any other type of seal, sometimes reaching depths of 5000 feet (1524m) when searching for prey. Perhaps surprisingly, considering their smaller size, females dive deeper than males. Both sexes can stay underwater for up to two hours, due to the incredible capacity of their blood and muscles to hold oxygen, and their ability to function at depth with a greatly slowed heart rate.

The Ross, Weddell, crabeater, leopard and southern elephant seal are all so-called 'true' seals, unable to move out of water except by shuffling their bodies. Antarctic and sub-Antarctic fur seals, on the other hand, are far more mobile on land. They, in common with all other 'eared' seals, including sea lions, use their flippers to lift their bodies up off the ground and can virtually walk. Fur seals once lived in huge numbers around the Southern Ocean but they were hunted mercilessly in the 19th century for their pelts, which were used to make coats and other clothing. Both species were driven right to the brink of extinction and today their colonies are shadows of what they once were. Thankfully, however, they are recovering well, with their numbers doubling every five years or so.

Fur seals are also found in the Bering Sea and the Sea of Okhotsk, which are filled with pack ice for part of the year. The species is different – these are northern fur seals – but their appearance and behaviour are similar. The Bering Sea is joined by the Bering Strait to the Chukchi Sea, which is part of the Arctic Ocean proper. Fur seals do not venture this far north. The Arctic Ocean is inhabited only by true seals and another, related creature, the walrus.

The walrus is virtually unique so scientists classify it in a family of its own. Although it has some physical features in common with seals, in many ways it is very different from them. The most obvious difference in terms of appearance is that the walrus has tusks. Both sexes bear these, although they are longer and thicker in males. Walruses feed on different prey from seals, digging up clams and other shellfish from the sea bottom. They find their food with the help of many bristly whiskers, which cover the top lip. Walruses have long been noted for their ability to squirt jets of water from their mouths. It is thought that they do this on the sea bottom to expose hidden prey.

Walruses are very social animals, both in the water and out of it. They haul out on ice floes and rocky beaches, sometimes in huge numbers, to rest. Often, they are packed so closely together that some individuals actually find themselves lying on top of others, but this rarely causes conflict. If anything, these large animals seem to enjoy the close physical contact, dozing contentedly in the warmth of shared body heat.

Like many polar animals, walruses have a thick layer of bodily fat, known as blubber, for insulation. They also conserve heat while in the water by contracting the blood vessels near the surface of their skin. This gives them a pale appearance when they first come out of the sea, but they quickly return to their more familiar reddish brown.

Walruses share the Arctic Ocean with five species of seal. The largest of these is the hooded seal, which grows to more than ten feet (3m) long and can weigh as much as a third of a ton (335kg). The hooded seal gets its name from the male's bizarre hood, which covers the top of its head. This is inflated to intimidate rivals during aggressive displays. The male hooded seal can also force the lining of its nasal cavity out through one nostril, blowing it up like a big red balloon.

Hooded seals are generally solitary but gather together to moult and to breed. The females haul out on to ice floes to give birth and have the shortest lactation period of any mammal. The pups are weaned just four days after they are born and follow their mothers to hunt fish in the sea.

Other Arctic seal pups take longer to become independent, but as long as they are unable to swim they are vulnerable to attack from polar bears. Ringed seal mothers try to protect their pups by hiding them in snow caves. As the winter pack ice thickens and snow starts to build up on its surface, the pregnant females dig up though the ice from below and hollow out chambers in the snow. Here they give birth to their pups and keep them for two months until they are weaned. The females are able to enter the water from their caves to hunt and only return to the pups to feed them. As well as hiding their pups from view, these snow caves also give them some protection from the cold: although they have long, fluffy coats, ringed seal pups take some time to build up a thick layer of blubber.

Harp seals and ribbon seals give birth out on the ice. The only protection their pups have is the camouflage created by their white fluffy coats. Both species have much shorter lactation periods than ringed seals, reflecting the greater urgency they have getting their young into the water. The fifth Arctic species is the bearded seal. Its pups are born with more conspicuous greyish-brown coats, but are able to swim within a few days of birth. When hauled out on the ice, the bearded seal tends to stay close to the edge with its head hanging over the water and the wind blowing from behind it. This position ensures that it gets advanced warning of any approaching threat from the ice. It also means that if the seal does pick up the scent of danger it can quickly escape to the safety of the sea.

The seals of the Arctic clearly spend a lot of their time in fear of attack and they have good reason to be afraid. This part of the world is home to the world's largest land carnivore, the polar bear. Standing on its hind legs, an adult male polar bear can be over 11 feet (3.3m) tall. The biggest on record weighed in at just over a ton/tonne.

Polar bears are solitary hunters that wander the pack ice in search of prey. Their main food is seals, which they catch out of the water, creeping up until they are in range, then charging in before they can make their escape. The bears find food in the vast white wilderness by using their incredible sense of smell. This is so acute that it can even pick up the scent of ringed seal pups hidden beneath snow. If a polar bear should come near enough to a ringed-seal den to detect it, there is usually only one outcome. By rearing up and crashing down on its front paws, the bear gradually bludgeons its way in. Unless the pup is old enough to escape into the water, its fate is sealed. Polar bears also hunt by lying in wait next to the breathing holes seals make in the ice, then grabbing them when they come up for air.

Although they are really land animals, polar bears are excellent swimmers and they have no hesitation in entering the water to reach new ice floes. They paddle with their forepaws, dragging their hind limbs behind. Polar bears' feet are partially webbed and their white coats are water-repellent. If necessary, these carnivores can swim steadily for several hours.

Left: *A polar bear sniffs the water's edge for the telltale scent of seals. Polar bears live almost exclusively on seals, which they hunt on the pack ice lying over the Arctic Ocean.*

Above: *The white coat of a harp seal pup provides it with both warmth and camouflage in the few days before it is able to swim.*

Previous pages: *A walrus rests on floating ice. Walruses are confined to Arctic waters.*

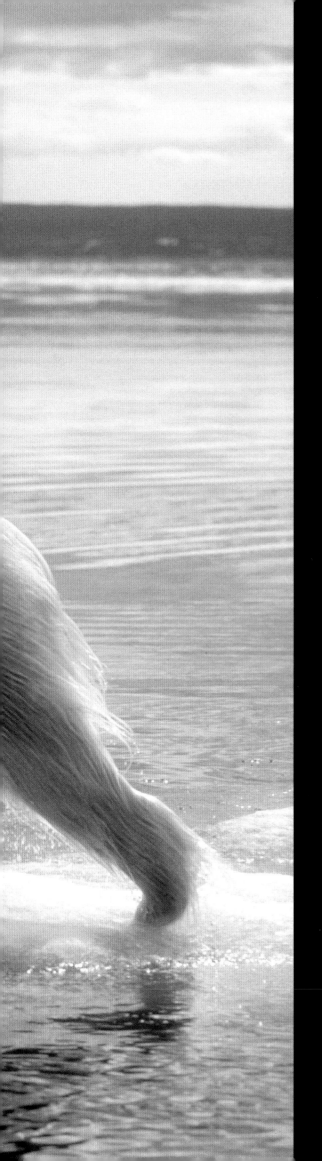

Left: A polar bear emerges from the sea. Polar bears are excellent swimmers and often swim long distances to reach new ice floes in search of prey. They paddle with their front paws, which have webbing between the toes, and use their hind legs to steer.

Top: A young southern elephant seal emerges from the water. Elephant seals are great divers and sometimes hunt more than a mile beneath the surface.

Above: Bearded seals rest on slabs of floating ice in the Arctic Ocean. This species is named after its long white whiskers.

Under the ice

While conditions can vary widely above the surface, temperatures under the water never drop below 28.6°F (-1.9°C). Upwelling and the continual horizontal movement of water prevent the Arctic and Southern Oceans freezing solid, even when they are covered by a crust of ice. The Arctic Ocean extends right over the North Pole. Although in winter one could walk from Canada to Russia across its ice-cap, submarines – and fish – can also make the journey unimpeded in the waters below.

The relatively stable temperatures in polar waters make them less forbidding to life than they might at first seem. Nevertheless, they do present animals with particular challenges. While phytoplankton abound in summer, during the dark months of winter there is far less to eat. Many polar fish and crustaceans are thought to migrate to more temperate latitudes in winter to avoid this problem, but there are others that stay behind. Some feed on dead and dormant phytoplankton, as well as organic detritus and hardy algae that live on the underside of the ice. Others hunt these small, tough grazers.

In the Southern Ocean the food chain is sustained mainly by krill. In summer, these shrimp-like crustaceans form vast swarms in open water which draw in huge numbers of larger creatures to feed. Those krill that do not migrate survive the winter by eating the meagre pickings on the underside of the ice sheet. While they usually find enough to sustain them, they are unable to grow. Indeed, some are forced to digest their own body tissues and decrease in size before spring. Krill also wait out the winter as eggs lying on the seabed. When the sun returns, they hatch and swim up into the shallows to find food.

Sea water freezes at a lower temperature than fresh water because it contains salt. This presents fish with a serious problem: how to prevent ice crystals forming in their blood. Many fish avoid it by leaving the area in winter when the water is coldest but others have evolved a way to cope, enabling them to live and feed below the ice all year round. These fish survive by producing a natural antifreeze in the form of organic chemicals known as peptides and glycopeptides. These circulate as part of their blood, lowering its freezing temperature below that of the surrounding sea water, so ensuring that it stays as liquid. They are so effective that some fish are even able to live within the ice itself, excavating burrows as places of refuge from predators.

It is not just fish and krill that spend the winter in polar waters: some marine mammals live here all year round too. In the Antarctic crabeater seals spend the winter hunting beneath the ice. At this time of year they have to work extra hard to keep their breathing holes open because the water's surface freezes even faster than usual. Other seals move north with the extending pack ice as winter takes hold, along with the killer whales that hunt them.

Both here and in the Arctic there are permanent holes in the ice sheet where the water remains open all year round. These holes are known as polynia and they act as refuges for air-breathing creatures, places where they can wait out the winter if cut off from the open ocean by the advancing ice. Most polynia are kept open by upwelling currents. These carry slightly warmer water and keep the surface in continual motion, both of which help to prevent ice from forming.

Elsewhere, huge cracks in the ice sheets, known as leads, act as channels along which marine birds and mammals can travel. These are kept open more by the movement of water in horizontal currents near the surface. Leads enable air-breathing animals to travel and hunt much nearer the poles than they would otherwise be able to do. In the Arctic they are often used by belugas and narwhals. These small whales, which are closely related, are only found in this part of the world. Both feed on fish, squid and krill in open water and under the ice. Belugas are also known as white whales and sea canaries. The latter name is a reference to the great repertoire of sounds they produce, some for communication and others as part of their complex and sophisticated system of echolocation. These moos, clicks, trills, squeaks, twitters and whistles can often be heard above the surface as well as below it.

Narwhals are famous for their long tusks, which are often said to have been the inspiration for the legendary unicorn. The function of these is uncertain, although they are thought to be used by the males much as stags use their antlers, to assert their dominance over younger, weaker rivals and to fight with those against which they are evenly matched. Certainly, most old male narwhals have scars around their heads that look like they were inflicted by tusks.

Page 240: Although it is more common in the temperate coastal waters of the north Atlantic, the grey seal ranges up to the southern limits of the pack ice in winter.

Page 241: A humpback whale breaks the surface in Antarctica's Fournier Bay. Humpbacks travel to the Antarctic in summer in large numbers to feast on the huge swarms of krill.

Above: *Divers enter the Southern Ocean through a hole in the ice. Below them circle four crabeater seals, creatures of elegance that move with effortless ease in the water.*

Left: *Krill live in the Southern Ocean all year round. As spring returns and the sun spends more time in the sky, the algae on which krill feed bloom and their numbers soar.*

The majority of adult male narwhals have a single tusk, although some individuals have two. Females, generally speaking, do not possess them although there are occasional exceptions to this rule.

Narwhals and belugas can be found in the Arctic Ocean all year round. They share its waters in winter with three other cetaceans: the killer whale, the minke and the bowhead. The bowhead is by far the largest creature to overwinter in polar waters. A close relative of the right whales, it spends its whole life in the Arctic Ocean and the neighbouring waters of Baffin Bay, the Bering Sea and the Sea of Okhotsk. The bowhead feeds almost entirely on krill and it has the longest baleen plates of any whale at well over 10 feet (3m) from base to tip. It gorges itself in summer and survives the winter mainly by living off its fat reserves.

Although polar waters are surprisingly busy with life in winter, in summer they positively teem with it. Phytoplankton blooms in clouds so dense that they can be seen from space and this feeds vast shoals of krill and small fish. Around both poles, the bounty draws in great numbers of

***Opposite:** A pod of male narwhals travel through the Arctic Ocean. The long 'horn' on the head of each narwhal is actually a modified tooth, which pierces the upper lip. Narwhals are occasionally seen in mixed groups but it is more usual for them to be separated by sex.*

***Below:** Polar bears often swim with their heads underwater, only lifting them above the surface to breathe.*

blue, minke and humpback whales. Sei whales also make the journey, although they tend to avoid the pack ice and gather in the open waters just beyond its edge. Grey whales travel to the Chukchi and Bering Seas in spring to feed. Like all of these migratory whales, they give birth during winter in warmer waters, which are better for their calves.

Around Antarctica, penguins start to venture farther south as spring returns. Female emperors trudge across the ice to relieve their starving partners and other species begin to return to their traditional nesting colonies. The long days of the short summer are filled with the frenzied efforts of parents to feed themselves and their growing chicks. Eventually, with the onset of autumn, they return to the sea, along with their newly fledged offspring.

The world beneath the permanent ice is almost as mysterious as the deep sea. Few people have ever travelled here and even fewer have stopped to look at the life-forms these waters contain. The only regular passages made beneath the Arctic ice-cap are undertaken by nuclear-powered military submarines. The sea beneath the Antarctic ice cap has even fewer visitors.

In recent years, however, exploratory dives have been made under the Arctic ice by remote-controlled unmanned submersibles. These have shown that these waters are full of life. In summer, ice algae grow on the underside of the ice sheet like mould on a damp ceiling. One species hangs down in green strings like submarine Spanish moss. These and the phytoplankton in the water feed zooplankton, which, in turn, are eaten by larger invertebrates such as copepods. They are fed on by larger animals such as Arctic cod.

The waters below are home to jellyfish and several types of squid. In fact, the world's largest jellyfish is found beneath the Arctic ice. Known as the lion's mane jellyfish, it has a bell diameter of up to 8 feet (2.4m) and tentacles that that grow to over 100 feet (30m) long.

Jellyfish are not the only giants beneath the Arctic ice cap. This is also the home of the world's second-largest predatory shark, the Greenland, or sleeper, shark. The Greenland shark grows to almost 18 feet (5.4m) long and can weigh well over a ton/tonne. Most of the time it moves slowly to conserve energy but when it needs to attack it is capable of frightening bursts of speed. It is anything but a fussy eater, consuming a wide range of prey. One Greenland shark was found to have the entire body of a caribou in its stomach.

As well as hunting both beneath the ice and in open water, the Greenland shark scavenges the bodies of whales and other animals on the seabed. To be found throughout the water column is a rarity among sharks – most species are either shallow or deep water specialists. However, the Greenland shark has geography in its favour: the Arctic Ocean is by far the world's shallowest, with an average depth of less than 4000 feet (1219m).

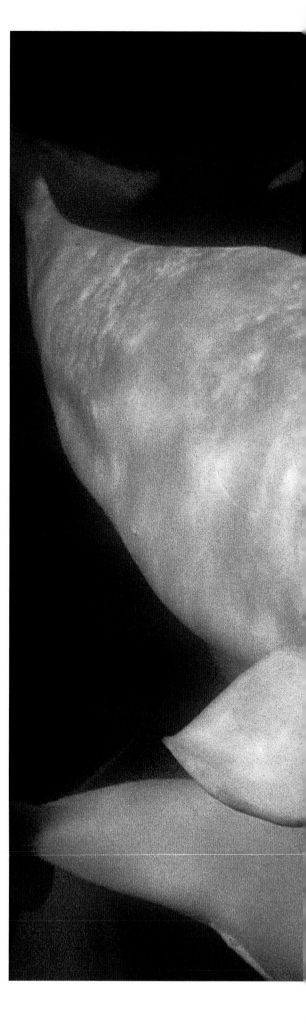

Previous pages: Belugas are sociable animals which live and travel in groups. They are unique among whales in being able to change their facial expressions, pursing their lips and altering the shape of the forehead when vocalizing.

Above: Small icebergs, known as growlers, sit stranded by the tide in Hudson Bay.

Right: A king penguin at sea. Penguins use their stiff wings as paddles to 'fly' underwater and steer with their feet.

Left: Like the grey seal, the harbour seal ranges north into icy waters. In Britain this species is known as the common seal, despite the fact that it is rare in British waters compared with its cousin.

Previous pages: Humpback whales have lumps like giant callouses on their heads and flippers. These provide anchorage points for barnacles, which spend their adult lives attached to the whales.

Top: In Arctic waters the lion's mane jellyfish grows to a colossal size. Like most other jellyfish, it feeds on fish, which it catches with its stinging tentacles.

Above: An Antarctic cod swims at the ocean's surface. This is the second longest and heaviest of all Antarctic fish species, growing to 5 feet (1.5m) in length and weighing an average of 55lb (25kg).

Index